Plastics

GREAT INVENTIONS

Plastics

NORMAN H. FINKELSTEIN

 Marshall Cavendish
Benchmark

New York

Marshall Cavendish Benchmark
99 White Plains Road
Tarrytown, NY 10591-9001
www.marshallcavendish.us

Text copyright © 2008 by Marshall Cavendish Corporation

Library of Congress Cataloging-in-Publication Data

Finkelstein, Norman H.
Plastics / Norman H. Finkelstein.
p. cm. —   (Great inventions)
Summary: "An examination of the origin, history, development, and societal
impact of the development of plastics"—Provided by publisher.
Includes bibliographical references and index.
ISBN-13: 978-0-7614-2600-4
1. Plastics—History.   2. Plastics—Environmental aspects.   3. Plastics
industry and trade.   I. Title.

TP1116.F56 2007
620.1'923—dc22
2006020909

Series design by Sonia Chaghatzbanian

Photo research by Candlepants Incorporated

Cover photo: Tim McGuire/Corbis

The photographs in this book are used by permission and through the courtesy of: *Hagley Museum and Library*: 2, 13, 51, 54, 65, 68, 94, 108. *Corbis*: Serge Kozak/zefa, 8; Bettmann, 11, 16, 23, 45, 33, 62, 64, 81, 87; Daniel Attia/zefa, 14; 19, 49, 89; Brigitte Sporrer/zefa, 21; Envision, 28; Underwood & Underwood, 30; Alen MacWeeney, 35; DK Limited, 38, 70; Estelle Klawitter, 42; PhotoCuisine, 46; Steve Prezant, 72; Jim Zuckerman, 78; Randy Faris, 79; Neil Guegen/zefa, 85; Laura Dwight, 96; Jan-Peter Kasper/dpa, 99; Goldberg Diego/Sygma, 101; Richard T. Nowitz, 105; China Photo/Reuters, 110; Tony Latham/zefa, 116; Richard Hutchings, 119; Roger Ressmeyer, 91, 122. *Getty Images*: 25, 40, 83; Time Life Pictures, 61, 75, 113, 115. *The Image Works*: ©NMPFT/Daily Herald Archive/SSPL, 56; ©SSPL 59.

Printed in Malaysia

1 3 5 6 4 2

CONTENTS

Plastics

PLASTIC CONTAINERS, SERVING A VARIETY OF USES, CAN BE FOUND IN A NEARLY ENDLESS ARRAY OF SIZES, SHAPES, AND COLORS.

Paper or Plastic?

"I just want to say one word to you. Plastics."
—*The Graduate*, 1967

Put this book down and look around you. Unless you are on a desert island, you will probably see something made of plastic. Perhaps it is the watch on your wrist or the pen in your pocket. It might be the television against the wall or the lamp on a table. Perhaps it is that DVD you are about to watch or the iPod® funneling a tune into your ears through a plastic earpiece. Plastic is everywhere. We may often take the benefits of plastic for granted yet cannot imagine life today without it.

Can you think of a world without plastic? When personal effects were recovered from the passengers on the *Titanic*, which sunk in the frigid North Atlantic Ocean in 1912, not a single item found was made of plastic, not even a button or a comb. Today, a century later, plastic is inescapable—in automobiles, airplanes, and trains, in homes, offices, and schools. Every day we use hairbrushes, toothbrushes, plastic wrap, and ketchup bottles. Plastic is in our computers and wraps our candy bars. We carry groceries in plastic bags and use other plastic bags to dispose of our trash, which includes other items made of plastic. Disposable diapers have made babies' lives dryer and parents' lives easier. Children play with Barbie® dolls and Legos®, Silly Putty® and Ping-Pong balls. And to pay for it all, we use plastic credit and debit cards instead of cash. Can you think of an aspect of your daily life in which plastic does not play a role?

The widespread use of plastic did not begin until the middle of the twentieth century. Today, more plastic is produced in the United States than steel. As we look back, we can directly trace today's wondrous advances in electronics, space exploration, food packaging, and health care to the discovery of this amazing synthetic substance. According to the definition in the *Oxford American Dictionary and Thesaurus*, plastic refers to "any of a number of polymeric substances that can be given any required shape, as by molding it under pressure while heated." Although synthetic plastics date back only to the nineteenth century, reference to natural plastic materials can be found much earlier. In the Bible, Moses's mother built a basket to hide the infant among the reeds of the Nile River. She "caulked it with slime and pitch," which acted as a natural waterproofing by filling in the basket's various openings and small holes.

The word *plastic* comes from the Greek word *plastikos*, referring to any pliable material that can be shaped or molded by heat or pressure or a combination of both. Over centuries, people learned to use natural materials such as plant fibers, animal skins and horns, amber, and clay to form utensils and bowls and to create waterproof coatings.

Natural plastics were used by early civilizations and were commonly traded by Phoenician and Greek merchants. In modern times, scientists used the insights gleaned from common knowledge and scientific experiments to improve and expand the types and properties of plastics. Resinous secretions from insects such as shell lacca (used to make shellac) were used as protective coatings for fine art and furniture. Shell lacca was widely used from the early 1800s, when it was molded into small cases and picture frames, to the 1940s when it was used as a popular insulator for radio and electrical components. By the 1840s gutta-percha, a natural gum collected from trees in Malaysia, was being used to mold knife handles and as a waterproof covering for underwater cables. Another form of natural plastics used in earlier times was animal based. Horns, hoofs, and tortoise shells were common materials that could be melted, crafted, and shaped into a variety of products.

POLYMERIZATION IS A PROCESS THAT COMBINES MANY SMALL MOLECULES TO FORM COMPLEX MOLECULAR UNITS. BUTADIENE AND OTHER INGREDIENTS THAT ARE USED IN THE PRODUCTION OF SYNTHETIC RUBBER ARE POLYMERIZED IN LARGE STEEL VESSELS, WHERE THEY ARE AGITATED AND EMULSIFIED UNDER PRESSURE IN A SOAP SOLUTION. THE PROCESS RESULTS IN THE CREATION OF MATERIAL WITH A MOLECULAR STRUCTURE SIMILAR TO THAT OF NATURAL RUBBER.

Turning from the realm of natural materials, twentieth-century chemists learned to create synthetic compounds of plastic using hydrocarbon molecules from such substances as natural gas, petroleum, and coal. These small molecules or monomers are chemically bonded to form longer chains called polymers or plastic resins. Different combinations of monomers yield resins with special properties and characteristics such as hardness or flexibility. Other chemical agents, called plasticizers, are added to produce specific plastics for specific needs. Most of the plastics in use today were developed over the past seventy years using variations in the basic chemical process to create a wealth of products ranging from soda bottles to bowling balls. Plastics have a unique ability to be processed into any imaginable shape, in almost any texture and color without additional finishing work required. Once a particular mold is fashioned, identical plastic products can be duplicated in any quantity.

The way in which polymer molecules form bonds determines the physical properties of the resulting plastic material. While plastics share a certain trait, each resin has its own attributes that make it suitable for specific uses. Whether the material is flexible or rigid, a foam or a solid depends on the arrangement of the molecules. Abraham Lastnik, a plastics expert, described the chemical makeup of plastic in human terms. "Imagine if you will that each molecule is a person. If you then add additional people, holding hands they form a polymer. The group can then be herded into various shapes or designs."

Until the 1920s, chemists and tinkerers experimented and built on one another's discoveries. From their work the new plastics industries emerged. Over time, different "families" of specialized plastics have been created each with special characteristics. Even within these individual families, the introduction of a single additive can give a specific plastic a totally new look and use. Polyurethane, for example, is best known as a clear protective coating in liquid form. With the addition of a plasticizer additive, it can be turned into a soft car seat.

Depending on the specific production process, plastic can be formed into a variety of complex shapes yielding such diverse products as shrink-wrap, toys, pens, medical devices, and store signs. Through the use of dies and molds, any number of identical plastic products can be produced. Other plastics can be spun, creating artificial fibers and

PLASTIC HAS CHANGED THE AMERICAN HOME PERHAPS MORE THAN ANY OTHER SUBSTANCE.

PLASTICS HAVE REVOLUTIONIZED THE MANUFACTURE OF SPORTS EQUIPMENT, MAKING IN-LINE SKATES SAFER AND MORE DURABLE.

fabrics that have changed the way we dress. Garments containing polyester and other synthetics provide protection from dirt while being easier to maintain. Next time you go shopping for clothes, check the content labels to see just how much of your potential purchase is composed of artificial fibers.

Plastics have changed the way we live. In our homes, plastics have made our refrigerators more energy efficient while giving us more usable interior space without increasing the appliance's overall size. And if you are hungry, look inside. Leftovers are covered in plastic wrap or kept fresh in reusable plastic containers. Thirsty? Your milk or favorite soda or juice is available in plastic bottles.

According to an article in the *New England Journal of Medicine*, bicycle helmets made from plastic reduce the risk of head injury by 85 percent. In-line skating would not have been possible without the use of a variety of plastics, some of which add rigidity while other forms provide flexibility and the low-friction wheels. Plastics also protect us. Bottled medicines and many food products have plastic tamper-proof bands that assure safety. Police officers wear bulletproof vests made of high-tech plastic. These accessories have saved the lives of more than two thousand law enforcement people. In our local hospitals, disposable plastic items help to maintain a sterile environment. Plastic incubators have helped save the lives of premature babies.

Slowly throughout the first part of the twentieth century, the plastics revolution began. The new substances began to compete with more traditional materials such as wood, metal, and glass. As the price of plastic items dropped and quality improved, demand for plastic-based products grew. By 1955 *House Beautiful* magazine stated, "The news is not that plastics exist, but [that] they have already been so assimilated into our lives."

CHARLES GOODYEAR WAS AN AMERICAN INVENTOR AND THE ORIGINATOR OF
VULCANIZED RUBBER.

From Plants to Plastic

"The teeth do not explode."
—*The New York Times*

It was probably Christopher Columbus who introduced rubber (or latex, the sap of the rubber tree) to Europe. From its initial appearance, people expressed interest in this amazing new material that was elastic and flexible. A major drawback, they soon discovered in Europe's often cold damp climate, was the effect extremes of temperature had on the substance. Hot weather turned the rubber sticky and smelly, while cold weather made the substance too brittle for any practical use. In 1839 an American, Charles Goodyear, made a pivotal discovery when he accidentally spilled a mixture of latex and sulfur on a hot stove. When the mixture cooled, he scraped it off and found that the rubber had become stronger and more elastic. More importantly, it remained flexible in hot and cold temperatures and resisted chemicals that would ordinarily cause it to dissolve. Vulcanized rubber, as Goodyear called it, led to a variety of uses such as tire production and waterproofed clothing. It was the first time a chemical had been used with a natural polymer (in this case, rubber) to produce a material that could be molded. With the advent of bicycles and the automobiles that followed, this discovery proved invaluable.

Samuel F. B. Morse's mid-nineteenth-century invention of the telegraph brought the world closer together. Even as telegraph lines spread across the United States and vast stretches of Europe, a major obstacle remained. How could people on one continent communicate with those across the vast Atlantic Ocean? Without a reliable material that was waterproof and could provide electrical insulation, laying an underwater telegraph cable would be impossible.

The discovery of gutta-percha proved to be a timely solution. Experimenters found that the rubberlike material could serve as the perfect wire insulator for an underwater cable, since unlike rubber, cold temperatures did not adversely affect it. During the American Civil War, gutta-percha and vulcanized rubber were made into raincoats, blankets, and canteens.

Natural polymers had been used for centuries to create molded materials. Amber, tortoise shells, and animal horns could be heated or shaped into a variety of useful objects including handles, combs, jewelry, and ornamental objects. But those materials were expensive and, because they were found only in nature, of limited availability. With the discovery of chemical ways to improve or imitate natural polymers, luxury goods previously available only to the wealthiest individuals became within reach of a wider range of consumers. Vulcanized rubber and gutta-percha, however, proved to be only the beginning.

The story of modern plastics is largely a tale of accidental discoveries. Some experts say it began in England in the 1850s with the work of Alexander Parkes. Parkes was an inventor and chemist who was fascinated by the properties of collodion, a material derived from nitrocellulose and also an ingredient used in explosives. Collodion was in widespread use as a liquid coating for cuts, scrapes, and surgical incisions. Once spread onto the wound, it sealed the area and kept out germs, allowing the wound underneath to heal. It proved to be an indispensable part of medical kits used during the Civil War. In Parkes's investigations, by a process of trial and error, he heated a mixture of nitrocellulose and camphor. To his delight, he discovered that the substance, while still in a plastic state, could be molded or shaped.

Parkes's discovery of this initial form of celluloid marked the first time anyone had succeeded in creating a material that imitated the look, feel, and shapes of valuable items made out of natural plastics.

IN THE 1850S THE ATLANTIC SUBMARINE CABLE MADE INSTANT COMMUNICATION BETWEEN THE UNITED STATES AND EUROPE POSSIBLE. A GUTTA-PERCHA COATING, WHICH PROTECTED THE CABLE FROM UNDERWATER CORROSION, WAS KEY TO THE PROJECT'S SUCCESS.

Parkesine™, as he called it, was publicly displayed to great acclaim in 1862 at the Great International Exhibition in London, where it was awarded a bronze medal. Parkes hoped his discovery would become a commercial success as a cheap and bountiful replacement for two popular but expensive natural plastics then in use—rubber and gutta-percha. He had initial success in manufacturing decorative brooches and handles for mirrors and knives. But due to the lack of funds, he had used inferior materials that caused his products to lose shape or even melt in hot weather. His company went bankrupt within a few years even as others tried to correct the flaws in his work.

Credit for perfecting Parkes's original discovery goes to an American, James Wesley Hyatt. Hyatt was a young printer with an interest in inventing. He had been experimenting with nitrocellulose when he heard of a tempting contest. A leading American manufacturer of billiard balls was offering a $10,000 prize to anyone who could come up with a substitute for ivory. The elephant population of the world was rapidly dwindling as hunters killed them for their tusks. Ivory was the invaluable component of piano keys, jewelry, as well as the only source for billiard balls. While Hyatt did not enter the contest, he accepted the challenge and set to work. He came up with a number of models using a variety of substances, but none could reproduce the heft, feel, and sound of real ivory.

It was then another accidental discovery that propelled the history of plastic to its next phase. One day, while in a printer's shop, Hyatt opened a cabinet and found that someone had spilled a bottle of collodion on a shelf. Collodion had been discovered in 1846 by a French chemist who was experimenting with ether, a form of alcohol, as a solvent for nitrocellulose. The resulting sticky solution quickly became used as a glue and lacquer coating. Already in use as a protective covering for wounds, printers coated their fingers with it to shield their hands from the heat of the lead type they used. The pliable but tough residue left by the spilled material intrigued Hyatt. The result was a billiard ball that mimicked real ivory. In 1869 Hyatt patented the use of collodion as a coating for billiard balls. There was, however, one small but disturbing problem. Players using the new balls quickly discovered that when the balls hit one another, the impact caused small explosions. The possibility of fire and the unease it caused among billiard players sent Hyatt back to the laboratory to rethink his discovery. He remembered Parkes's use of camphor and a year later patented a new process for creating a material using nitrocellulose and camphor. He had developed a product he called celluloid, the first commercially successful semisynthetic plastic able to be molded under heat and pressure into a shape it retained after it cooled. Celluloid opened the world to the endless possibilities of the plastic age.

JOHN WESLEY HYATT'S EXPERIMENTATION WITH COLLODION LED TO ITS USE AS A SUBSTITUTE FOR NATURAL IVORY, GREATLY ALTERING THE WAY BILLIARD BALLS WERE MANUFACTURED.

Soon Hyatt and others began manufacturing a wide array of products made out of celluloid. In Leominster, Massachusetts, the "comb capital of North America," celluloid began replacing natural horn and tortoise shells as the basic materials for combs and other decorative items. The new semisynthetic material was easier to carve, polish, and color and, of course, manufacturers were especially drawn to it as it was easier to produce and much less expensive than natural plastics. The world's remaining elephants, tortoises, and whales were given new leases on life.

Some of the most popular uses of celluloid were as false teeth and as detachable shirt collars, fronts, and cuffs. In 1827 a Troy, New York, housewife got tired of washing her husband's shirts to get the collars clean. So she removed the collars and washed them separately, before reattaching them. The detachable collar became a standard of men's fashion for close to one hundred years. Originally, many were made of linen and had to be frequently washed and ironed to near rigidity. Celluloid made wash days easier. A plastic collar could be produced in any style or texture and had the added convenience of always retaining its shape. A damp cloth could take care of smudges, dirt, and even lipstick. The only drawback was the discomfort the wearer experienced when he turned his head too suddenly, causing the rigid collar to pinch his neck.

Another early use for celluloid was in the manufacture of dentures or false teeth. Dentists had been using rubber. The substance's moldable properties made it possible to create dentures that fit individual patient's mouths. Celluloid did the same job at a much lower cost. But there were drawbacks. Celluloid denture wearers had to cope with a permanent camphor odor (like mothballs) and the reality that celluloid lost its shape when heated. Drinking a hot cup of tea could cause the dentures to warp. Some wearers even reported that their teeth sparked when they bit down sharply on a hard candy or nut. Denture wearers were more than pleased when later nonexplosive plastics ultimately replaced celluloid.

Celluloid was also used extensively in making women's grooming sets consisting of combs, brushes, handheld mirrors, and cosmetic containers all on a decorative tray. The Fiberloid Company was a leading producer of the popular items. One of its advertisements proclaimed: "Good taste shows itself unerringly in dressing table appointments. Fiberloid appointments in which every color you select, in toiletware that will add a last touch of distinction to the room it so fitly [sic] completes. In many varied colors, its wide selection of patterns and decorations makes it possible for you to choose the right toiletware for your dresser." Today there are only a few consumer items still made of celluloid, notably guitar picks and Ping-Pong balls.

Have you been to the movies lately? Or have you taken a photograph with a film-based camera? You can thank James Wesley Hyatt for making that possible. Before celluloid, taking a photograph was cumbersome and involved the use of heavy chemically treated glass plates. When George Eastman learned about celluloid, he realized that it could revolutionize photography. In 1889 he used cellulose nitrate coated with photographic chemicals to produce the first flexible photographic roll film that fit into a small camera. The rest, as they say, was a Kodak moment. Going one step further, in 1891 Thomas Edison added sprocket holes to the flexible and transparent celluloid film and invented the motion picture.

GEORGE EASTMAN REVOLUTIONIZED PHOTOGRAPHY WITH HIS INVENTION OF ROLL FILM, CELLULOSE NITRATE COATED WITH PHOTOGRAPHIC CHEMICALS.

Remember the exploding billiard balls? They were also made of cellulose nitrate. Eastman's film proved to be flammable too. The early history of movie theaters is filled with stories of disastrous fires that took many lives when the film being run through a projector overheated and burst into flames. Other people died in flash fires at celluloid factories. In 1908 George Eastman created "safety film" made from cellulose to which acetate, instead of nitrate, had been added.

Chemists, tinkerers, and inventors soon found other uses for cellulose, as once again spilled collodion led to an intriguing discovery. A young chemist, the count of Chardonnet, began wiping up a collodion spill and noticed that strands of the substance stuck to the cloth. The thin fibers reminded him of the strands of natural silk. He immediately set to work finding a silk substitute. In 1884 he was finally able to produce a fabric from cellulose that appeared to have many of the properties of real silk. Chardonnet's discovery became known as rayon, the first artificially manufactured fiber.

Before the silkworms could retire, though, the flammable nature of cellulose nitrate surfaced once again and initially compromised the new fabric's success. Wearing an imitation silk dress made a fashion statement, but having it burst into flames while you were wearing it was another story. It took a while longer to discover that substituting cellulose derived from cotton rather than wood and using acetate instead of nitrate made the artificial material far less flammable. Chemists quickly developed other forms of artificial silk. The viscose process is the one most widely used today in the manufacture of rayon. It involves batch processing of purified cellulose in a series of steps including steeping, pressing, ageing, filtering, spinning, and cutting to create ultimately rayon. The advent of chemical modifiers in the 1940s made high-performance rayon an important component of automobile tires.

These early successes with synthetic material led to additional experimentation with even more diverse substances. In Germany, a chemist accidentally discovered that by treating a milk derivative called casein with rennet and other additives, he was able to produce a substance that could be easily molded. Because of its ability to be produced in many colors and with a lustrous finish, it became a popular substitute for horn and ivory in the making of buttons and buckles.

The use of natural polymers, such as horn, rubber, and gutta-percha, and semisynthetics, such as cellulose-based products, marked the true beginnings of the modern plastics age. Today, most plastics are derived from chemicals or petroleum and provided to factories where they are used to manufacture products. In the early stages of manufacture most plastics are monomers, composed of small single molecules, but under the influence of heat, pressure, or chemical catalysts, these small

DR. HERMANN STAUDINGER IS CONSIDERED THE FOUNDER OF POLYMER CHEMISTRY. HE WAS AWARDED THE NOBEL PRIZE FOR CHEMISTRY IN 1953.

molecules combine to form the long-chain polymer molecules that make up solid or semisolid structures. This process is called polymerization. The idea that polymers were made up of giant chains of molecules was first suggested by a German scientist, Dr. Hermann Staudinger, in 1917. His work led to further advances in plastics in the twentieth century. In recognition of his theory, he was awarded the Nobel Prize in Chemistry for 1953.

Other ingredients, plasticizers, which determine the flexibility, texture, coloration, and the heat- and light-retention properties of a final product, may be added. Chemical companies produce the plastic resins—liquid polymers—and the molding powders or pellets that manufacturers use to create their products. The processing procedures in use today are based on those developed years earlier. Plastics are created under heat and pressure and converted into finished products by one of several methods.

Extrusion is a continuous process in which molten plastic is forced out of a long heated chamber through a small opening into a mold or die to be cast in the shape of the desired product. It is often used to create plastic tubing and bags.

Blow molding is used with the extrusion method to form a molten tube of plastic inside a mold. Then, compressed air is blown inside the tube to expand it against the walls of the mold. This method is used to create hollow products such as soda and milk bottles.

Injection molding uses a closed mold into which molten plastic is pushed. Once the plastic is cool enough, the mold opens and the finished product is ejected. This is one of the most widely used processes and is employed to create containers for yogurt and butter.

Rotational molding consists of a mold placed on a swivel, which allows it to move in several directions. Molten plastic can then be distributed uniformly. Large hollow products such as kayaks and certain toys are formed using this process.

Spinning is the process used to produce polymer fibers. The polymer is heated until it flows. It is then pumped to the face of a spinneret, a metal disk containing many small holes. The streams of polymer that emerge, called filaments, are formed into a long fiber that can then be spun into textiles and clothing.

There are two basic plastic forms. **Thermosets**, the first fully synthetic plastics, remain rigid once they are molded and set and will not soften when heated. Once shaped, further refinements have to be made by machine. Examples of thermosets are Bakelite, polyester, polyurethane, and products such as radio and television cabinets and cases housing telephone circuitry. **Thermoplastics** are the second form. They can be reshaped when reheated. Examples are nylon, polystyrene, and polyethylene, which together form most of today's popular plastic products, such as bottles, plastic wrap, cups, and household appliances. An additional form, **elastomers**, has fewer molecular crosslinks than thermosets, producing a degree of elasticity. Like thermosets, elastomers cannot be reshaped by heating. A major use of elastomers is in the manufacture of automobile tires.

There are thousands of different plastics in use today. Nearly all fall into one of the six major categories as described by the American Plastics Council. Within each category, the resulting plastic products may vary depending on the plasticizers and additives added to create unique applications or to enhance specific qualities.

Polyethylene terephthalate (PET or PETE) is clear and tough, making it ideal for soft drink and medicine bottles. Because of its ability to withstand high temperatures, it is also used to form heatable pre-prepared food trays. In other forms, it is found in the fibers of clothes and carpets and in applications for which precision molding is required.

High-density polyethylene (HDPE) is used to make milk, water, and detergent bottles since it displays excellent moisture-barrier properties and chemical resistance. Other applications are as cereal box liners, molded yogurt and margarine tubs, and detergent containers.

Polyvinyl chloride (PVC) can be divided into rigid and flexible materials. In rigid forms, it is used extensively in construction for siding as well as water and sewer pipes. Because of its transparency and chemical resistance, it is also ideal for containers for cooking oil, meat wrappings, and medical tubing.

Low-density polyethylene (LDPE) is the most commonly used plastic. Its transparency and flexibility make it ideal for use in dry-cleaning bags, grocery bags, and for protective films. It is also used for flexible lids and bottles.

Polypropylene (PP) is frequently used in packaging and, because of

PLASTIC BOTTLES HAVE BECOME THE CONTAINERS OF CHOICE FOR STORING SOFT DRINKS AND WATER. THEY ARE LIGHTWEIGHT, SHATTERPROOF, AND RECYCLABLE.

its high melting point, is perfect for holding or storing hot liquids. It can be formed in rigid, flexible, or fiber forms making it a popular choice for such varied applications as condiment bottles, medicine bottles, diaper linings, and carpets.

Polystyrene (PS) is a versatile plastic that can be rigid or foamed. Its clarity allows it to be used when transparency is needed, particularly in medical and food packaging. In its foamed state, it is shaped into egg crates, coffee cups, and dehydrated soup containers. The owners and patrons of take-out restaurants appreciate the properties of polystyrene containers, both foamed and molded, which are lightweight, strong, and able to retain heat.

Together, these various plastics revolutionized life, starting in the twentieth century and extending to today. Plastic may have had an accidental history when it came to its formative years, but it was an innovation that was destined to stay. Durable, flexible, and affordable, plastic proved to be an indispensable aspect of modern life.

AMERICAN CHEMIST LEO BAEKELAND CREATED THE FIRST THERMOSET PLASTIC, BAKELITE, WHICH HE NAMED AFTER HIMSELF.

Baekeland's Astonishing Discovery

"The material of a hundred uses."
—A Bakelite Corporation slogan

According to an old saying, necessity is the mother of invention. The relatively short history of plastics is filled with instances that clearly show how one discovery can lead to advances in other non-related areas. By the turn of the twentieth century, companies were producing new inventions and appliances based on electricity. Ignition systems for automobiles, film projectors, and electricity-based household items required quality insulation. An important factor limiting the growth of the electrical market was the lack of a natural insulation material—usually shellac or hard rubber—in sufficient quantities to meet the demands of growing innovation.

The search for a viable substitute for shellac was well under way at the beginning of the twentieth century. One of the experimenters was Belgian-born chemist Leo Baekeland. A wealthy man after the 1899 sale of his Velox® photographic printing paper to the Eastman Kodak Company, Baekeland set up a sophisticated laboratory in the stable of his Yonkers, New York, home. There, drawing on the work of earlier European chemists, Baekeland set out to find a substitute for shellac. The amber-colored resin he produced by the chemical reaction created by combining phenol and formaldehyde turned out not to be synthetic shellac, but yet another kind of electrical insulator that just happened to be a new form of plastic. It was a liquid resin that hardened rapidly and took the shape of any container that held it. Baekeland had invented the first synthetic plastic. It was able to withstand high temperatures, moisture, and chemical reactions. Yet, unlike other plastics, once it was molded, it could not be melted and re-formed. It remained solid. He made this discovery public in 1909.

Others had experimented with phenol and formaldehyde, but Baekeland took their work one step further by heating the mixture of the two substances under pressure. He invented an ugly egg-shaped 6-foot-tall (1.8-meter) contraption he called the Bakelizer to do the job. Plastics historian Jeffrey L. Meikle said it "symbolized the moment when Baekeland ceased being a researcher and began being a businessman."

His General Bakelite Company quickly transformed the way many existing products were made while opening the door to new ones. From Parker pens to Kodak cameras, Bakelite was the key ingredient. The original Bakelizer was presented to the Smithsonian Institution National Museum of American History in 1983.

Oxybenzylmethylenglycolanhydride, the chemical name for Baekeland's discovery, was the first fully synthetic plastic. It displayed properties previously unknown in cellulose-based plastics. Baekeland, perhaps recognizing the difficulty in pronouncing his discovery, simply named it after himself, calling it Bakelite. A few years later, John Wesley Hyatt substituted the new material for cellulose in his popular billiard balls. Not only was Bakelite cheaper than cellulose, it was much easier to mold to specific sizes and shapes than previous plastics were. It also had the added benefit of not exploding. Furthermore, Bakelite could be machine molded, making it possible for items to be mass-produced. The American Chemical Society said, "Bakelite set the mold for the modern plastic industry."

According to the *Bakelite Review*, "As early as 1912 there were hundreds of uses and applications for Bakelite materials. There were cast resinoid materials for fancy articles, smoking pipes, cigarette holders, costume jewelry and the like; varnishes for electrical insulation . . . ; lacquers for protecting metallic objects—brass bedsteads, chandeliers and

THOMAS EDISON WAS RESPONSIBLE FOR THE INVENTION OF THE MICROPHONE, THE MOTION PICTURE CAMERA, AND THE PHONOGRAPH.

hardware; . . . cements which resisted moisture, steam, soaps, acids, solvents and heat . . ."

The first major use of Bakelite was in electrical insulators. Shellac and hard rubber, the materials most widely used, deteriorated from the heat produced by electrical equipment. Bakelite did not. It retained its shape irrespective of temperature or exposure to solvents. It did not crack, soften, or fade. It quickly lived up to its motto, "The Material of a Thousand Uses." Thomas Edison used it to make phonograph records that would not melt or easily shatter. By the 1920s Bakelite was used in electrical switches and sockets, telephones, radios, cameras, ashtrays, and the handles for kitchen appliances. Still, the most widespread product made out of Bakelite was the standard, now outdated, black telephone. No matter what shape the telephone took well into the 1960s, Bakelite was used to make it.

The engines on early gasoline-powered automobiles had to be started via a hand crank. The invention of an automatic ignition system can be partially credited to the existence of Bakelite, a workable insulation material immune to the effects of heat, moisture, oils, and acids. In 1895 there were just four automobiles registered in the United States. In 1934 there were close to 22 million, featuring more and more plastic parts. By 1918 Bakelite could be found throughout many vehicles, in the form of radiator caps, gear shift knobs, battery terminals, door latch handles, and gas tank covers. By the 1930s the list expanded to include instrument panels, ignition locks, ash trays, cigar lighters, heaters, and radios.

On November 2, 1920, KDKA, a radio station in Pittsburgh, began the first scheduled broadcasting of programs. Within three years, more than six hundred stations were broadcasting across the United States. As radio's range expanded, demand for the era's simple radio sets grew with it. Radio followed Edison's creation of the phonograph decades earlier. Both innovations were dependent on an unending supply of shellac, a coating derived from the secretions of the lac beetle. Reliance on the insect became intensified since shellac was an important component of producing recordings and electrical goods. With all the electrical advances, the poor beetle just couldn't keep up.

A July 31, 1926, article in *The Science News-Letter* declared, "With the radio replacing the phonograph in almost every home, the shellac shipments from India into this country are only half of what they used to be two years ago. At least half of the shellac used in the United States, which is one of the biggest importers of this necessary constituent of varnish, formerly went into the manufacture of phonograph records, according to a report to the American Chemical Society."

DURING THE 1920S, BAKELITE'S MALLEABLE PROPERTIES LED TO ITS USE IN THE
PRODUCTION AND DESIGN OF A RANGE OF ITEMS INCLUDING RADIOS AND CLOCKS.

Bakelite was also featured in these increasingly popular consumer products. Because Bakelite imitated wood in looks, it soon became a good substitute for wood and was used to finish the interiors of automobiles and to mold cabinets for radios. Radio cabinets could be manufactured as single units, in a variety of colors, and formed into appealing designs at a fraction of the cost of the wood cabinets they replaced. Because Bakelite was molded, designs and patterns could be automatically included, eliminating the expense of hand labor. For people living through the Depression years of the 1930s, affordable Bakelite radios brought entertainment and news into their homes. When World War II broke out in 1939, the abundance of inexpensive radios made it possible for citizens to keep up with the events transpiring abroad. Advances in the casting of Bakelite and other phenolics also made it possible to produce stylish radio cabinets in a variety of colors.

Not only was Bakelite cheaper than wood, its ability to be molded into eye-catching designs made it instrumental in creating the streamlined art deco style that marked the 1920s and 1930s. Leading designers looked to Bakelite as a means of improving design and increasing the salability of their products. With the emphasis on streamlined shapes, vibrant colors, and simple forms, Bakelite was an obvious choice. *Business Week,* in a 1935 article, stated, "modernistic trends have greatly boosted the use of plastics in buildings, furniture and decoration, and contrariwise, plastics by their beauty have boosted modernism." Bakelite and similar plastic materials enhanced the popularity of art deco building and decorating styles. The ability to laminate or mold the plastic with rounded edges and complex shapes added to the streamlined aerodynamic effect. Rounded contours provided protection against breakage. A noted designer of the time said, "out of the union of art and industry one thing has been born—beauty of design. It is beginning to be accepted as a practical necessity in industry."

During the Great Depression, people of all financial backgrounds could afford to purchase inexpensive yet stylish jewelry and radios molded out of Bakelite. Costume jewelry, made to look like valuable substitutes for diamond, silver, and gold pieces, has existed since the nineteenth century. The Bakelite jewelry developed in the 1920s offered a totally different look and appeal. The bright colors and the ease with which it could be shaped allowed the imagination of jewelry designers to soar. Customers were pleased. Its affordability made luxury-like goods available to those with limited incomes, while the wealthy enjoyed the sophisticated, durable, and glamorous styling. In a 1927 advertising stunt, a Parker pen molded of Bakelite was dropped 23 stories to a concrete sidewalk below and endured the fall intact.

Baekeland's discovery was considered so revolutionary that he was featured on the cover of *Time* magazine in 1924. The accompanying article dramatically praised Bakelite.

> Superficially, it is a composition, born of fire and mystery, having the rigor and brilliance of glass, the lustre of amber from the Isles. Poetically, it is a resin formed from equal parts of phenol and formaldehyde, in the presence of a base, by the application of heat. It will not burn. It will not melt. It is used in pipe stems, fountain pens, billiard balls, telephone fixtures, castanets, radiator caps, etc. In liquid form, it is a varnish. Jellied, it is a glue. Those familiar with its possibilities claim that in a few years it will be embodied in every mechanical facility of modern civilization. From the time that a man brushes his teeth in the morning with a Bakelite-handled brush, until the moment when he falls back upon a Bakelite bed all that he touches, sees, uses will be made of this material of a thousand purposes.

In 1927 the Bakelite patent was acquired by the Catalin Corporation, which added colors to the original formula and expanded the popularity of molded items, particularly small radios.

Durable and adaptable, Bakelite proved to have many practical uses, and its growing popularity led to the development of several new products. Its balance of strength and rigidity appealed to furniture manufacturers. Its electrical insulation properties aided the development of an array of safe electric switches and switch boxes. Its ability to withstand

BAKELITE'S ABILITY TO WITHSTAND CHEMICALS AND HEAT MADE IT A POPULAR CHOICE FOR THE MANUFACTURE OF TELEPHONES AND ELECTRICAL DEVICES.

high temperatures made it an ideal choice when producing the handles of kettles, cookware, and irons. Its resistance to moisture pointed to its use as agitators in washing machines, and its resistance to solvents and chemicals resulted in its being formed into film developing trays.

Next time you brush your teeth, look at the cap of your toothpaste tube. Give it a turn. The cap comes off easily so you can squeeze toothpaste onto your brush (made of plastic, of course). Before Bakelite was used to fashion the first plastic caps for tubes and bottles, manufacturers had to rely on other types of closures, usually made of metal. The obvious problems were corrosion, which made containers difficult to open, or a less than tight seal, which allowed the contents to spoil or dry out. Some old containers called for the strength of Hercules to open them. With Bakelite, manufacturers could precision-mold caps to fit their containers. As the Bakelite Company boasted, "Trademarks and distinctive designs could be readily incorporated. Lightness in weight and resistance to chemicals offered additional advantages. Unusual shapes—special sprinkler tops, useful 'measuring cup' closures—all were made possible through the magic of molding art. A new and basic packaging trend was established!"

In many homes today, kitchen counters appear as if they are made of granite or other natural stone. If you look closer, you will discover that the counters are actually covered with a laminated plastic such as Formica®. The use of synthetic material to imitate natural grain and texture grew with the popularity of Bakelite. Developed in the 1930s, laminated forms of Bakelite became widely used not only in homes but in businesses as well. Restaurants liked the clean, sanitary surface while banks and offices welcomed the streamlined, smooth look. Bakelite provided a feeling of modernity.

Remember the shocking problems that faced the wearers of false teeth made out of celluloid? Bakelite came to the rescue. As described in the *Bakelite Review,* "The dental profession was demanding a product that would not have . . . shortcomings but would contain all of the properties required in a good denture material." In 1933 Bakelite introduced

Picture Post, 27 March

You deserve a 'Formica' kitchen

...and extra help in every room

THIS 1954 ADVERTISEMENT EXTOLS THE VIRTUES OF FORMICA®-BRAND PLASTIC LAMINATES IN KITCHENS.

Luxene, a pink translucent resinoid denture material. It combined strength with translucency, surface hardness with reparability. And, unlike older celluloid false teeth, it did not spark and did not melt when the user drank hot beverages.

Bakelite was the first fully synthetic plastic. But it would not be the last. There was now no turning back. Chemists around the world realized the implications of this revolutionary material and accepted the challenge of creating other forms of plastic. The innovations that followed gave rise to the plastic age, an era we are arguably still living in.

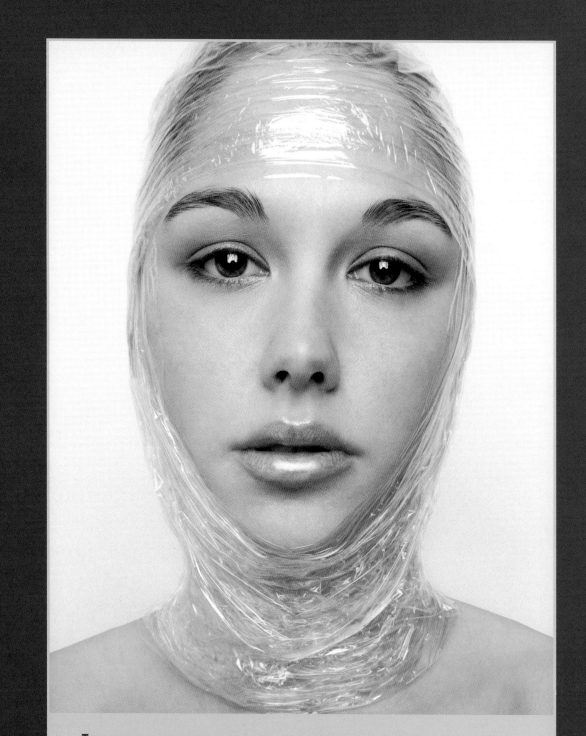

The novelty of plastics, much less their flexibility and transparency, led some designers to investigate the use of different plastics in fashion.

FOUR

You're the Top! You're Cellophane

"Better Things for Better Living, through Chemistry."
　　　—DuPont slogan

When Wallace Carothers left a teaching position at Harvard University in 1928 to work for the DuPont Company, little did he realize the impact he would soon have on the plastics world. A year earlier, DuPont began a mission to discover "new scientific facts" and expand its already successful plastics businesses. Executives built and funded a state-of-the-art facility for "pure scientific research," which quickly became known as Purity Hall. DuPont's philosophy was simply stated in a 1935 employee magazine, "No day passes that modern chemistry doesn't help make life happier and more complete for them—and for you." While Carothers and his team of scientists experimented with ways to synthesize polymers, another plastic material was already "on top" of the world—cellophane.

DuPont had previous success with cellulose-based material. In the early decades of the twentieth century, the company successfully marketed a leather substitute made of pryoxylin, which they called Fabrikoid, for automobile seats. Unlike natural leather, their synthetic material resisted grease, oil, perspiration, and mildew and was less expensive than the real thing. Now cows could join the growing list of animals whose lives were extended by the wonders of plastic. A DuPont advertisement explained, "Cow production could hardly keep up with car production . . . so leather men were finding it difficult to meet with demand for automobile upholstery material . . ." Plastics once again provided an economical and practical alternative to natural materials.

The history of plastics in the twentieth century emerged as a story of intuition and experimentation, as scientists began creating a growing list of other plastics, each with its own unique qualities and applications. At dinner one day in 1904, a Swiss chemist, Dr. Jacques Brandenberger, watched a diner accidentally spill red wine on a tablecloth. He wondered what would result if the cloth had been infused with a transparent flexible film that could just be wiped dry. He returned to his laboratory and set to work. Eight years later, he produced a cellulose-based mixture he called viscose, a form of rayon. Viscose, however, only made cloth brittle. Taking another route, Brandenberger forced the viscose into thin slots to form sheets. In 1912 he patented his process for producing cellophane.

When its first use as a replacement for camera film failed—it melted when heated and, being made of cellulose and nitrate, it easily exploded—World War I came along and provided a successful application. The use of fatal mustard gas against opposing forces required well-designed gas masks to repel the toxic fumes. Cellophane came to the rescue. It proved to be the perfect filter. It provided a barrier to the poison gas while not fogging up the lenses so soldiers could see clearly.

After the war ended, the DuPont Company bought the rights to viscose and cellophane and set out to broaden the applications of cellophane to include everyday practical uses. One of the problems with cellophane was its inability to resist moisture. After a few years of experimentation, DuPont chemists finally produced the first batch of moisture-proof cellophane in 1927. Its first commercial use was to wrap boxes of Whitman's chocolates.

Next time you go to the supermarket, try to count how many products you see wrapped in cellophane-type material. At the meat counter, row after row of poultry and cuts of meat sit neatly wrapped in individual trays covered with see-through plastic. In the cookie aisle, many boxes are wrapped the same way. In the produce aisle, you can pick up

BEGINNING IN WORLD WAR I, PLASTICS ENTERED THE BATTLEFIELD. HERE, AMERICAN
SOLDIERS ARE WEARING GAS MASKS CONTAINING PLASTIC LENSES.

PLASTIC PACKAGING OF FRESH FRUITS AND VEGETABLES PROVIDES SHOPPERS WITH CONVENIENCE AND CLEANLINESS.

sealed plastic bags of lettuce and plastic containers of herbs.

Seventy years ago, grocery shopping was an experience much different from what it is today. Supermarkets were rare, and shopping was done in specialty stores. There were neighborhood stores for fish, bread, meat, fruit and vegetables, and packaged groceries. Stephen Fenichell, in *Plastic: The Making of a Synthetic Century,* recalled that food was touched by "strange hands, inquisitive hands, dirty hands, touching, feeling, examining the things you buy in stores." Cellophane changed the way we buy food.

It led to the development of unit packaging. No longer did you have to wait for the butcher to cut a steak or two. Now you could choose packages of the desired weight with see-through coverings. A DuPont brochure announced, "Cellophane protects you from dirt's danger. It is on the job, protecting your health and your pocket book." The president of DuPont's cellophane division told *Forbes* magazine, "Madame Consumer wants to see what she buys and she wants it clean."

In the 1930s it seemed that people, still adjusting to the novelty of the plastic wrapping, would buy almost anything sealed in cellophane. Sales of donuts actually increased when the bakers wrapped them in the transparent packaging. Cigars and cigarette packages were wrapped in moisture-proof cellophane to guarantee freshness and quality. Everything looked more appealing and fresh to shoppers when wrapped in the transparent material.

The well-known Cole Porter song "You're the Top," which extolled the wonders of the world, included the following lyrics prominently mentioning the new material:

You're the purple light of a summer night in Spain.
You're the National Gallery. [Washington's National Gallery of Art]
You're Garbo's salary. [Greta Garbo was a popular actress of the time]
You're cellophane.

Stephen Fenichell states that *Fortune* magazine listed some of the products of the 1930s that came wrapped in cellophane. They included violin strings, plated silver, golf tees, suspenders, shirts, hot-water bottles, shoelaces, spark plugs, tapioca pies, baby carriages, golf balls, pickles, clocks, and a deluxe edition of *The New York Herald Tribune*.

Richard Drew went to work for the Minnesota Mining and Manufacturing Company (3M) in 1921 where he invented masking tape. In 1930 another 3M scientist introduced Drew to cellophane. In a flash of inspiration, Drew envisioned adding adhesive to the waterproof cellophane to make a transparent sealing tape. The company's annual report for 1930 briefly mentioned its new product, Scotch™ brand cellophane tape. "Although it has many uses, its largest utility is sealing packages wrapped in moisture-proof cellophane. In view of the present popularity of cellophane as a wrapping medium, this market appears to have large possibilities." Selling a frill item such as Scotch™ tape at the height of the Depression may have seemed fruitless. Soon, however, people discovered uses for the new product that allowed them to prolong the life of their possessions. They could mend torn pages in books, seal open food cans, repair a child's broken toy, or affix labels to containers.

Across the Atlantic, chemists developed polymer materials of their own. In 1912 Fritz Klatte in Germany produced vinyl chloride (PVC) but did not know what to do with it. In 1926 an American, Waldo Semon, working for the B. F. Goodrich Company, independently rediscovered

PVC and its waterproofing ability. He thought it would make good shower curtains. PVC became one of the first plastics produced commercially. What made it so practical was its ability to resist two opposites: fire and water. A variety of uses were found for this new waterproof material including plumbing pipe, vinyl siding, and linoleum.

In England, chemists working at Imperial Chemicals Industries in 1932 accidentally discovered polyethylene. During one experiment featuring ethylene, a light gas made from petroleum, chemists found a "white waxy solid" on the walls of a reaction vessel. After months of additional research, they realized they had stumbled onto yet another new polymer. Polyethylene, a true thermoplastic, could be molded into any number of products by various techniques—injection molding, extrusion or casting. At first, researchers envisioned using polyethylene as an insulator in underwater cables. After opening a production plant, they discovered that the new polymer was better fitted as a unique insulation material to support the revolutionary invention of airborne radar. Because polyethylene was light and thin, radar could be placed aboard airplanes. This discovery came at just the right time. Radar became a valuable asset to the British and American armies fighting the Germans in World War II. Enemy bombers could be detected at a distance even through darkness and thunderstorms.

Polyethylene was kept secret until after the war when it emerged as a commercial product but with limited uses. In 1953 a German chemist, Karl Ziegler, discovered a method for creating polyethylene that was more rigid than the original product and could withstand heat. For his discovery, Ziegler received the Nobel Prize for Chemistry in 1963. Royston M. Roberts in *Serendipity* said, "It was one of Ziegler's principles to keep an eye open for unexpected developments and not to neglect new phenomena as irrelevant to the main project."

But even Ziegler's brilliant changes could not prevent consistency problems from emerging when it came to creating items out of polyethylene. While producers worked on ways to improve their products to benefit consumers, a new toy was introduced that saved the industry

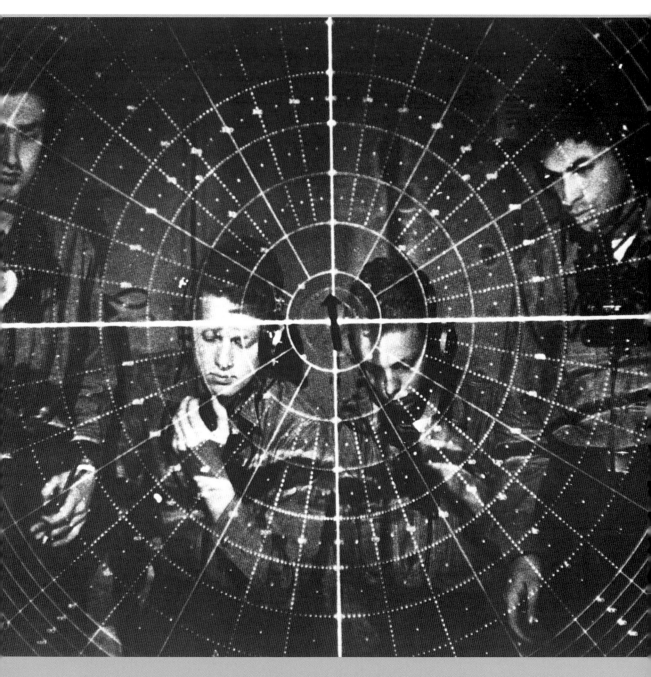

THE DEVELOPMENT OF RADAR TECHNOLOGY DURING WORLD WAR II WOULD NOT HAVE BEEN POSSIBLE WITHOUT THE AVAILABILITY OF PLASTIC INSULATION MATERIAL. HERE, MILITARY PERSONNEL WATCH A RADAR SCOPE FOR INCOMING ENEMY AIRCRAFT.

from financial ruin. Demand for hula hoops—circular pieces of polyethylene tubing that children and agile adults twirled around their hips—quickly claimed existing polyethylene stocks.

Another German discovery of the 1930s was Plexiglas®, an acrylic polymer. It found immediate use in the cockpit windows and canopies of military airplanes where its optical clarity, low weight, and shatter resistance made it an excellent replacement for conventional glass.

Back in Wilmington, Delaware, Dr. Wallace Carothers and his research staff would develop an innovation that would soon place another group of the world's animals in far less demand. This time, it was the wild boars of China whose bristles had been used for decades in making toothbrushes. The outbreak of World War II would limit access to these Chinese bristles.

Carothers had been exploring the properties of synthetic polymers. Other scientists had previously succeeded in accidentally producing synthetic molecules. Carothers ushered in a scientific breakthrough by purposefully manipulating molecules into specific fibers. In a moment of playfulness, a few scientists working with Carothers dipped a glass rod into the goo they had created. While one scientist held the glass beaker, another ran down the hall with the glass rod trailing thin threads of fiberlike strands behind him. The material Carothers created seemed to have qualities similar to natural silk. Unfortunately, the synthetic material melted at relatively low temperatures. After more tinkering, though, DuPont was ready to put the perfected fiber, called 6-6, into production. The number comes from the combination of six carbon atoms from diamine and six from dibasic acid. The raw material, today derived from petroleum, coal, and natural gas, is combined and heated so the molecules become superpolymers. Once cooled, the resulting material is ground into little chips. The chips are then melted and pumped through the holes in a spinneret. The width of the yarn is determined by the size of the holes. The size and texture of the resulting yarn depends on how many holes the melted material is forced through.

DuPont chemists and engineers developed manufacturing methods

THIS LABORATORY EXPERIMENT DEMONSTRATES THE MAKING OF NYLON, INSTANTANEOUSLY
AND AT ROOM TEMPERATURE, WITHOUT ANY EQUIPMENT OTHER THAN A GLASS CONTAINER.
THE CHEMIST SHOWS HOW A NYLON "ROPE" CAN BE DRAWN FROM A BEAKER.

for mass-producing this breakthrough, the first totally synthetic fiber. One of the DuPont scientists, Joseph Labovsky, an assistant to Carothers, described early experiments in *A Short History of Nylon.* "All spinning was done by the simple process of melting the new substance in a tube and forcing it out by means of gas pressure through a hypodermic needle." Eventually changes were made which allowed for mass production.

The first production plant was opened at Seaford, Delaware, in December 1939. A 1988 article in the *Leader and State Register* newspaper recalled that it took two years to settle on the name, *nylon,* which DuPont stated "is the generic name for all materials defined scientifically as synthetic fiber-forming polymeric amides, having a protein chemical structure: derivable from coal, air and water, or other substances and characterized by extreme toughness and strength and the peculiar property to be formed into fibers and into various shapes, such as bristles and sheets."

The first uses were as bristles on Dr. West Miracle Tuft toothbrushes—which, unlike boar bristles, did not shed or remain soggy—and in fishing lines and surgical sutures. Rumors quickly spread "miracle" claims for the new plastic. It was versatile, strong, and resilient and quickly became the world's most widely used plastic. In addition to its best-known form as a fiber, nylon could also be molded into such familiar durable items as pocket combs, mechanical gears, Velcro® fasteners, ski boots, shower curtains, umbrellas, and the strings of tennis rackets. Joseph Labovsky later said, "In nylon, we created a product that was more than a product—it was an industry, the plastics industry. It was one of the greatest commercial successes of the twentieth century." But its earliest success was focused on a seemingly unlikely use for a "miracle" plastic—women's hosiery.

At a highly publicized forum at the world's fair site in New York on October 27, 1938, DuPont proudly announced the "development of a wholly new synthetic material of hundreds of potential uses, one of which will be of revolutionary importance in fine hosiery. . . . Though wholly fabricated from such common raw materials as coal, water, and air, nylon can be fashioned into filaments as strong as steel, as fine as the spider's web, yet more elastic than any of the common natural fibers and possessing a beautiful luster." The audience of four thousand, most of whom were women's club members, burst into sustained applause. The idea of silklike stockings that were "strong as steel" captured their imaginations.

For decades, women had relied on silk stockings to complete their wardrobes. But silk stockings were expensive and had a tendency to "run." Any snag quickly led to unsightly rips and tears. The marketing professionals at DuPont knew that the average woman went through eight pair of silk stockings each year. So it was this market, adult females, that the company chose for its all-out sales campaign to familiarize the public with nylon.

The most popular exhibit at the 1939 world's fair was DuPont's Wonder World of Chemistry, featuring machines that knit nylon stockings while fairgoers watched. Young women paraded through the exhibit revealing to the curious onlookers their legs covered in the nylon stockings. Other models played "tug of war" with nylons to show the strength of the new stockings. Female consumers were hooked. The hype continued for another year as DuPont geared up to produce enough nylon to satisfy the anticipated need. The company arranged for trial sales in their home base of Wilmington, Delaware. A full-page Wilmington newspaper ad announced: WOMEN OF WILMINGTON ARE INVITED TO INSPECT AND PURCHASE THE STOCKINGS EVERYONE HAS BEEN TALKING ABOUT.

On Wednesdays, for six months, crowds of expectant women lined up outside Wilmington shops and department stores. Customers were limited to three pairs of nylon stockings and had to prove they were residents of the city. Interest in and demand for the hosiery skyrocketed. The frenzy was repeated on N-Day, May 15, 1940, when nylon stockings, or nylons as they are called, finally went on sale in selected stores across the country. Five million pair were sold in one day.

Just as nylons were becoming a nearly indispensable part of a

As part of a 1940s advertising campaign for nylon stockings, actress Marie Wilson, perched atop a crane, watched as a 2-ton 35-foot-high cast of her leg was unveiled in Los Angeles to promote the sale of nylons.

woman's wardrobe, the United States was attacked by Japan on December 7, 1941. That put a sudden end to both the availability of silk and the use of nylon for consumer purposes. Until the war ended in 1945, nylon was a war material employed in making hundreds of essential items from tires and tents to ponchos and military clothing. The most common use was in the manufacture of parachutes. Before the war, parachutes had been made of silk. With the silk markets under Japanese control, nylon's military importance rapidly increased.

Yet the growing demand for women's nylons could not be totally met, even with a war under way. Scams and thievery abounded. The bootlegging of nylons was reminiscent of the illegal liquor trade during the Prohibition era of the 1920s. Willing conspirators sometimes paid more than ten times the actual value of the forbidden item. An article reprinted in *Reader's Digest* in February 1945 cautioned, "Watch out for the fellow who offers to sell you 'nylon' hosiery! There isn't any." The article revealed a number of scams including one in which customers were sold a compound "which, dissolved in water, will 'nylonize' rayon stockings." Potential customers were told, "After the war there will be nylon hosiery, finer, sheerer, stronger, more beautiful than ever before. But until the war is over, the Army and Navy need every pound of nylon. So, ladies—don't be suckers."

But as patriotic as they were, many women still looked forward to the reappearance of the much sought items. A popular song by Fats Waller and George Marion Jr. (in their Broadway show *Early to Bed* and later in *Ain't Misbehavin'*), "When the Nylons Bloom Again," proclaimed, "I'll be happy when the nylons bloom again, cotton is monotonous to man." For the first half of the twentieth century and with the exception of certain products such as nylons, items made of plastic gained a reputation for shoddiness and cheapness. This was due to the newness of plastics, the wide availability of natural materials, and the fact that manufacturers were still experimenting with emerging polymer forms. It would take a war to enhance plastic's reputation.

PLASTICS' ABILITY TO BE EASILY MOLDED ALLOWED THE FAST AND ECONOMICAL PRODUCTION OF IDENTICAL CONSUMER GOODS THAT COULD BE SOLD AT AFFORDABLE PRICES. HERE THE WORKERS ON A FACTORY ASSEMBLY LINE PUT THE FINISHING TOUCHES ON RADIOS.

The Synthetic World Goes to War

"... a greater abundance of almost everything that adds to the
comforts and satisfaction of living—all these will be awaiting
the homecoming soldier when the war is won."
—Lammot DuPont, 1943

The way plastic successfully answered the material
needs of World War II not only improved the material's image and re-
ception but demonstrated that plastic products could have unique qualities that made them even better than the natural materials they often
replaced. Before the outbreak of the war, the plastics industry produced
a limited array of products—radio cabinets, decorative buttons, toys,
and other consumer items. A May 3, 1943, *Life* magazine article on
plastics heralded "war makes gimcrack industry into a sober producer
of prime materials." Gimcrack means showy, worthless, and flimsy, a
description not totally without merit for the pre-war period when plastics were often not respected by consumers and manufacturers.
Wartime technology changed that impression and turned plastics into a
respected family of unique materials.

Scientists drew on and expanded their existing knowledge of plastics technology to meet the special requirements of the war. Cheaper
to generate from materials that were abundant by-products of petroleum and coal, plastics replaced rubber, wood, and glass with synthetic
materials that, in many cases, surpassed the natural materials in their
performance. The production of civilian products molded from older
and familiar plastics such as Bakelite and Catalin™ was replaced by the

manufacture of items for defense needs such as military telephones and aviator goggles. This shift, however, did not prevent manufacturers from using other plastics, those not needed for military purposes, to produce substitute materials otherwise not available to the public because of wartime restrictions.

Even everyday toothbrushes were marketed with the war in mind. A 1943 advertisement for Pepsodent "50-tuft" toothbrushes—"made with Fibrex, DuPont's finest synthetic bristle"—cautioned, "With more and more men and women going into the United States military service, the importance of sound, healthy teeth is being particularly stressed by the medical and dental authorities."

Prior to World War II, an abundance of natural resources relegated plastics to a secondary position. Synthetic rubber, which was first developed in Germany, was considered a scientific curiosity of little practical importance. The world still depended on natural rubber, harvested mainly from the rubber tree plantations located throughout Southeast Asia. With the Japanese invading the region, Great Britain, the United States, and their allies found themselves cut off from a major source of the natural rubber that was essential for wartime needs.

In 1929 chemists working for Germany's I. G. Farben Company had patented a synthetic rubber that was formed from polystyrene, a copolymer made of two combined compounds—butadiene and styrene—which they called Buna S. But the costs connected with producing the product at a time when natural rubber was abundant and cheap, relegated it to a secondary role. In the mid-1930s two American rubber companies, Goodyear and Goodrich, began discussions with I. G. Farben to use the Buna S technology to produce tires. But the Germans, preparing for war, were secretive and withheld the information. The American companies conducted their own research without infringing on German patents but could not develop a realistic alternative to Buna S.

By 1940 the United States also knew it would soon be involved in the war and began an emergency project to develop synthetic rubber. The government formed the Rubber Reserve Company, which brought

THE PRODUCTION OF NATURAL RUBBER WAS TEDIOUS AND LABOR INTENSIVE.

university scientists and officials from rubber and petrochemical companies together, cutting through the "red tape" and professional jealousies which until then had delayed a timely production of synthetic rubber. Within two years, the researchers developed a polymerization process that resulted in a product even stronger and more resilient than natural rubber. The military need for tires was met, while the tire companies also looked to the possibilities present in the future, after the conclusion of the conflict. With tires for civilian use rationed, the General Tire Company urged the wartime consumer: "Imagine for yourself what new materials and processes may mean. Think of mileage that may outlast your car. Think of much less air pressure; no blowouts; lighter weight, yet more strength; the heat problem ended. True? You'll have to wait to see!"

The building blocks from which polymers are made were initially by-products of distilled coal tar. On the brink of World War II, chemists turned to petroleum and natural gas instead. Ethylene, from which polystyrene, polyvinyl chloride, and polyethylene are derived, was an abundant by-product in the refining of petroleum. America's petrochemical industry geared up to produce the large amounts of styrene needed to create synthetic rubber. Chemists began creating polymer substitutes for natural materials that would soon be in short supply. In a process called "cracking," larger hydrocarbons were broken into smaller molecules, a change that results in a variety of polymer forms.

With increased motivation from government and industry, American scientists, using test tubes and curiosity, created an arsenal of plastic-derived materials and fibers that proved essential to the war effort. Researchers quickly realized that identical chemicals could be molded into a large number of unrelated products. Cellulose acetate was turned into rayon; nylon was used to make parachutes and brush bristles; Vinylite® became imitation leather and fireproof insulation for ships' cables; Saran® was transformed into nonmetallic pipes.

In 1944 scientists at the General Electric Company developed a new material they called silicone rubber, made from silicon, a common and abundant component of sand and glass. The new synthetic rubber had important advantages over natural and other synthetic rubbers since it did not lose its elastic properties at either extremely high or low temperatures. While not suitable for use in tires because of that elasticity, one of its earliest wartime applications was as a gasket seal in large searchlights that housed high-intensity high-temperature electric-arc lamps. On land, these searchlights helped make approaching bombers more visible to gunners. On the water, powerful searchlights were just as invaluable for locating enemy planes. Furthermore, the silicone gaskets easily withstood the vibrations of a battleship's large guns.

Shortages of strategic materials such as aluminum and brass forced the military to turn to the plastics industry for substitutes. Soldiers used plastic bayonet handles, binocular cases, and even bugles. (After meticulous testing, the War Department discovered that the tone of the new plastic bugles even surpassed the original brass versions. The plastic version allowed 20 ounces [567 grams] of brass that would otherwise have gone into making the bugle to be allocated for more vital military needs). These human-made materials were often better, cheaper, and more adaptable, and they became as indispensable as bronze, gunpowder, and steel.

THE FLEXIBILITY AND TRANSPARENCY OF CERTAIN FORMS OF PLASTIC, SUCH AS VINYLITE®, LED TO NEW USES AND APPLICATIONS.

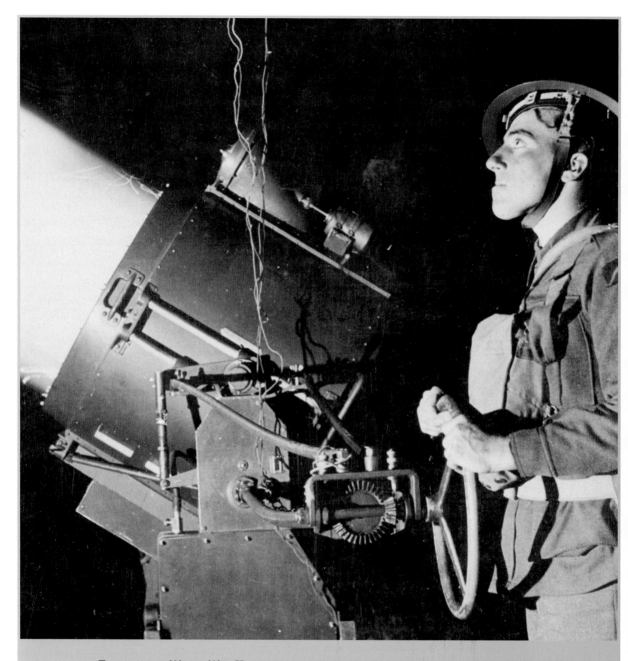

THE BEAMS OF WORLD WAR II SEARCHLIGHTS TRAVELED ACROSS THE SKY IN AN ATTEMPT TO SPOT ENEMY AIRPLANES. SILICONE RUBBER GASKETS, IMPERVIOUS TO MOISTURE AND HEAT, MADE IT POSSIBLE FOR THESE HIGH-INTENSITY BEAMS OF LIGHT TO SWEEP THE SKY FOR EXTENDED PERIODS.

The reality of life on the battlefield resulted in improvisations that led to procedural changes in many areas. Concerned with patients suffering often fatal infections from wounds, one doctor discovered that by adding medication to large sheets of cellophane tape, he could create a bandage that stuck to the skin for long periods. While some plastic innovations were life savers, others were not quite as successful. Drawbacks included plastic uniform buttons that melted during dry cleaning and rayon hosiery that had to be washed and dried in specific ways so that it would not shred or melt. Despite the drawbacks and necessary adjustments, though, when the war ended, soldiers, sailors, and aviators returned home with a new appreciation for the versatility of plastic.

The positive outlook led the DuPont Company to declare "The American chemical industry could be depended upon to do its part in keeping our soldiers and sailors well clothed for service, and the civilian population, too." To assure a common standard for the production of plastic items, the government set strict requirements that, as author Jeffrey Meikle states, resulted "in identical resins and interchangeable moldings from many different material suppliers and processors." Ironically, some of the key technologies were brought from Germany, where they had been developed in connection with the coal industry. Sometimes, the experimentation yielded unexpected results and yet another milestone in the development of the plastics industry. Of special importance was a new class of materials—thermoplastics—that could be remolded after heating thus allowing plastic products to be recycled for additional uses.

Other plastics entered the world stage in quick succession. The Rohm & Haas Company had already developed Plexiglas® resin, and the DuPont Company had invented Lucite®, both acrylics that are able to be easily molded into clear glasslike plastic. Lighter and tougher than glass, though, these acrylics could be fashioned into airplane canopies and gunner observation turrets for fighters and bombers, perfect replacements for heavy glass.

MADE OF DUPONT LUCITE®, THE FIRST PLASTIC ROWBOAT IS SHOWN ON ITS "MAIDEN VOYAGE" IN 1941. ALTHOUGH NEVER PUT INTO ACTUAL PRODUCTION, THE SEE-THROUGH CRAFT DEMONSTRATED THE STRENGTH AND TRANSPARENCY OF LUCITE®.

At the Pittsburgh Plate Glass Company, known today as PPG Industries, a team of scientists investigating clear resins created a compound, CR-39®, which led to the development of a major new industry called reinforced plastics. In liquid form, reinforced plastic could infuse layers of cloth and then be pressed between layers of plate glass. Once hardened, the boards could be used in a variety of ways, including as lightweight sections for an airplane's fuselage. A combination of CR-39® and fiberglass was key in the construction of lightweight fuel tanks for bomber airplanes, which not only reduced the plane's weight but extended the bomber's range.

Another innovative use of CR-39® in war planes was in the form of tubing that ran out of the fuel tank. This addition gave the flight engineer a visible gauge of the fuel flow to the engines. The new plastic tubing was a welcome change from the previously used glass tubes, which often shattered during combat, spraying gasoline throughout the cockpit.

Shortages of natural and synthetic materials led to government controls being placed on the manufacture and use of consumer items. In 1941 the War Production Board designated all nylon yarn reserves for military consumption. With the natural silk supply cut off from the United States, nylon became the indispensable substitute for the manufacture of parachutes, hammocks, and even shoelaces. As American troops found themselves fighting in inhospitable climates, ranging from frozen tundra to humid rain forests, the military could not get enough nylon, which, unlike the natural fibers it replaced, was resistant to mildew, heat, chemicals, and rot. At home, women donated their prewar nylons to help the effort. Highly publicized collection drives in American cities were so successful that tire manufacturer B. F. Goodrich Company praised American women in an advertisement, "We borrowed their Nylons to make tires for the Navy." Four thousand pairs of recycled stockings produced enough nylon cord to manufacture two bomber tires. Nylon-reinforced tires permitted heavy bombers to land safely on improvised airstrips while nylon flak vests protected soldiers from shell fragments.

LUCITE®'S PHYSICAL CHARACTERISTICS MADE IT IDEAL FOR USE AS NOSE CONES AND GUNNER TURRETS ON WORLD WAR II BOMBERS. IT WAS LIGHTWEIGHT, SHATTERPROOF, AND ABOVE ALL CLEAR.

Plastic earned a new reputation as it was put to new and practical uses. Yet even during the conflict, memories of cheap, easily broken prewar plastic devices caused public concern as to the safety and strength of military aircraft such as the Mosquito bomber. People began referring to these new aircraft as plastic planes, even though they were actually constructed of plywood—very thin sheets of wood bound with chemical adhesives derived from plastics research. The new material not only assured aerodynamic reliability but allowed planes to be built faster than using conventional methods and materials. The molded fuselages and wings were waterproof, much lighter than metal of the same strength, and without projecting parts on the exterior to interfere with air streams. The Interstate Aircraft Corporation took out advertisements to ensure a nervous public, "You have heard a great deal about plastic planes. Actually, there is no such thing and probably never will be." The advertisement went on to explain that by using plastic adhesives, traditional plywood could be molded into stronger and more durable airplane components.

Other materials, designed for use in creating consumer products, were easily transformed to suit military needs. Saran®, originally marketed by the Dow Chemical Company as a protective covering for theater seats, was prized for its use in the tropical regions as rot-free screens for keeping out insects. It also was successfully used to protect aircraft, engines, and other military equipment shipped overseas from exposure to the elements by hermetically sealing them and protecting them against air, moisture, and humidity. After the war, Saran Wrap became a popular covering for food. Dow also developed silicone, which as a solid proved to be an excellent electric insulator and as a liquid remained thick and gooey irrespective of extreme heat and cold. Styrofoam® or expanded polystyrene was used as insulation and protective packaging for a variety of military items. In block form, it was used to float equipment.

In an advertisement heralding the properties of its wartime Styron plastics, Dow Chemical, looking to the future, assured consumers that after the war, "all these properties point to one of Styron's largest potential fields—the American home." Similarly, other companies promised consumers the benefits of the wartime research efforts. Union Carbide and Carbon Corporation told readers of *Newsweek* magazine that through "research, American ingenuity, and patient development, scarce natural products have been duplicated or improved upon." The scientists promised better medicines created through synthetic chemistry and magic plastics that looked like glass, stretched like rubber, and resisted the often harmful destructive effects of water, sunlight, oil, and heat.

Prior to the Japanese attack on Pearl Harbor on December 7, 1941, the U.S. Army had become outdated and was ill equipped to fight a major war. The army's Quartermaster Corps had the task of organizing a force that would exceed eight million troops by the end of the war and that would be outfitted to fight in all possible climates and terrains. The corps quickly reallocated its funds to include the purchase of plastics, especially nylon and rayon, in the form of such disparate items as uniforms, mosquito netting, sleeping bags able to withstand extreme cold, knife handles, whistles, and canteens.

Responsible for more than 70,000 individual items, the Quartermaster Corps used intensive testing techniques to assure the quality of products provided to the troops. A *Time* magazine article reported that plastic canteens, for example, had to meet "higher standards than previous materials could meet. Tests included freezing the canteen while 90% full of water, dropping it ten feet onto concrete, tasting and smelling distilled water kept in the canteen 24 hours at tropic heat." By 1943 the Quartermaster Corp ordered all razor handles produced for the military to be made of plastic. Plastics were used innovatively both by Allied and Axis (German, Japanese, and Italian) troops on the battlefield. Early in the war, the Germans introduced a new kind of land mine made of plastic and concrete. Without metallic content, these mines were almost impossible to detect by traditional methods.

American manufacturers reconfigured their production lines to produce military equipment. General Motors and Ford transformed their automobile assembly plants to produce tanks while the Riddell Company, a manufacturer of football helmets, developed a liner for a helmet

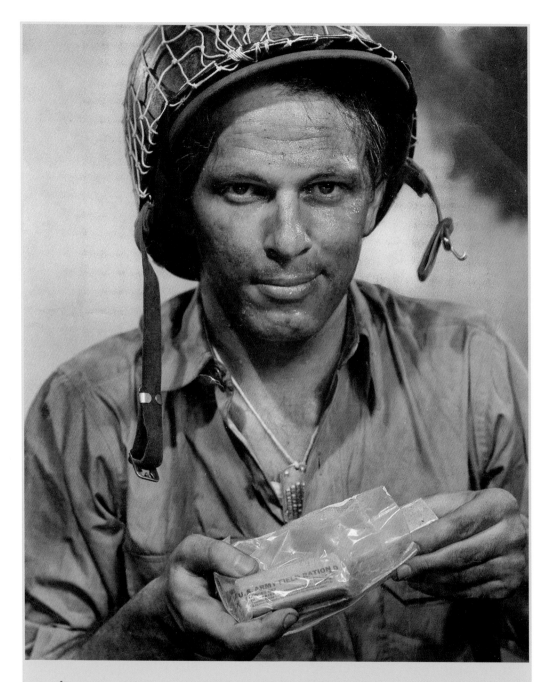

ALTHOUGH WE THINK OF CELLOPHANE AS EITHER A HOUSEHOLD TAPE OR A SUPERMARKET WRAP, THE COMMON COVERING WAS WIDELY USED DURING WORLD WAR II TO PROTECT DELICATE MILITARY EQUIPMENT AS WELL AS THE RATIONS SOLDIERS TOOK TO THE BATTLEFRONT.

suspension system. Using Vinylite®, a moldable plastic that could be shaped simply with hot water, John Riddell Jr., standing at a sink at Fort Benning, Georgia, formed a model of the liner that became the life-saving suspension system for the steel M1 helmet. By the end of the war, more than 50 million helmets had been manufactured. According to U.S. Army estimates, the newly designed helmet liner was credited with reducing battlefield casualties by 8 percent, saving an estimated 76,000 soldiers from death or serious injury.

On the home front, plastics not destined for military purposes were used to create substitute consumer items. During the war years, *The New York Times* ran a weekly column called "The Home in Wartime," which provided help to readers coping with shortages and rationed goods. In the columns, readers were told about new plastic utensils, garden hoses, and bridge or card tables made of non-priority plastic that were more durable than prewar models. They learned that because cellophane was needed for the war effort, wrappers would no longer cover playing-card boxes, candles, or lamp shades.

The development of Teflon® in DuPont's laboratories is a prime example of the way in which a combination of scientific curiosity and unexpected experimental outcomes can lead to a new discovery. Roy Plunkett was twenty-seven years old in 1938 when he became curious about a failed experiment using gasses related to Freon® refrigerants. As he examined a frozen sample of tetrafluoroethylene, he discovered that it had polymerized spontaneously into a white, waxy solid to form polytetrafluoroethylene (PTFE), a material that was unaffected by even the most corrosive chemicals and that was resistant to extreme high and low temperatures while possessing very little friction. It was, in fact, the most slippery material in existence. DuPont, at first unsure of the practical uses for this new material, patented Teflon® in 1941.

At the same time, scientists across the country were working on the ultrasecret Manhattan Project to develop an atomic bomb. At the Oak Ridge National Laboratory (known as the Clinton Laboratories until 1948), scientists seeking to create nuclear fuel for an atomic bomb

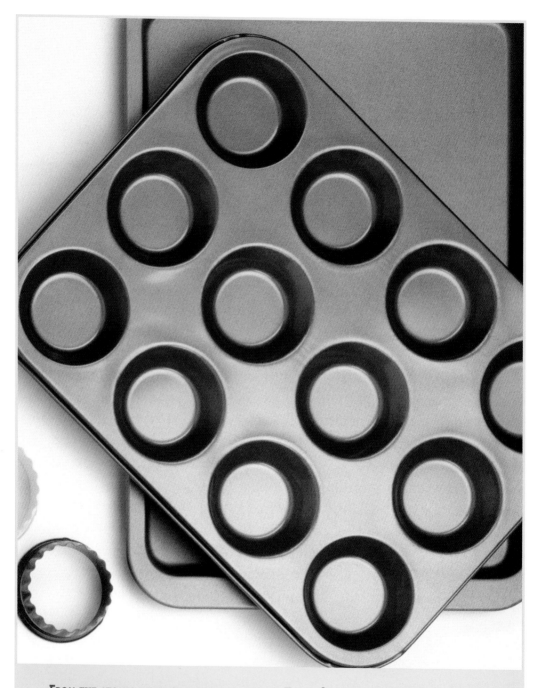

FROM THE ATOMIC BOMB TO KITCHEN BAKEWARE, TEFLON® PROVED TO BE JUST THE RIGHT SUBSTANCE WHERE A SLIPPERY SURFACE AND ANTICORROSION WERE NEEDED.

needed material that would not break up when it came in contact with corrosive elements. Plunkett's discovery provided the nuclear scientists with such a material. In 1944 DuPont began selling Teflon® to the military for use in the Manhattan Project. Other war uses for Plunkett's discovery, as noted by Stephen Fenichell, were as "coating for artillery-shell nose cones, an ideal insulation for radar wiring and storage liners for cold liquid fuel—so cold that conventional linings simply froze and turned brittle." After the war, Teflon® found many uses in the civilian world as a soil and stain repellent for fabrics and as a nonstick coating for cookware.

The dramatic advances in plastics technology during the war years set the scene for the future. At the height of the war, Lammot DuPont, chairman of the board of the DuPont Company, predicted that American chemical plants "would stand ready to turn out new plastics, new paints, new textile fibers, new fertilizers and a hundred and one other new materials in quantities undreamed of only a few years ago." He looked to the future and correctly forecast that airplanes "will be quadruple the size of the largest pre-war planes" and that the nation would be dotted with large airfields. At a 1942 meeting of the American Chemical Society, as reported in *The New York Times*, DuPont vice president Charles Stine said, "The war is compressing into the space of months developments which might have taken us half a century to realize if necessity had not forced the pace. Plastics will be available after this war on a scale beyond all previous conceptions." When the war ended, the techniques that produced Lucite® bomber noses and plastic laminated PT-boat hulls would be used to make refrigerators, chairs, automobile parts, and thousands of other applications not envisioned just a decade earlier. The plastic age had begun.

PLASTICS SOMETIMES WERE USED TO CREATE ITEMS ORIGINALLY UNFORESEEN BY CHEMISTS. ARTIFICIAL CHRISTMAS TREES, FOR EXAMPLE, HAVE BECOME POPULAR HOLIDAY STAPLES.

Better Things for Better Living

"Tupperware, what dreams are made of."
—Advertisement

After World War II, many people had high expectations for the peace-time uses of plastic. The war had proved that plastics could not only substitute for existing materials such as wood and steel but could also be fabricated for unique applications previously unimaginable. (Think about the soon-to-be brisk trade in plastic Christmas trees.) Roy Plunkett's discovery of Teflon® in 1938 greatly enhanced the war effort, and by the 1960s DuPont began producing Teflon® as a popular nonstick coating for baking and cooking utensils. Even as older plastics such as Bakelite continued to be molded into cookware handles, radio cabinets, and, beginning in 1948, television cabinets, consumers were ready to reap the benefits of a growing supply of synthetic goods after years of deprivation and shortages. Advertisements by national companies during the war had urged patience. "We do know that when this war is over B. F. Goodrich will offer you far better tires than ever built before Pearl Harbor." Through the wonders of science, new synthetics arrived to bring people, according to DuPont's famous slogan, "better things for better living through chemistry." Within a short time, wartime standbys such as Teflon® and Plexiglas® joined polyester, acrylic, Mylar™, and dozens of other newly invented fibers and resins to create consumer-oriented products.

The successful uses of Plexiglas® during the war led to peacetime applications as well. Clear plastic's ability to be bent and shaped through heat expansion at first led to its appearance in cheap novelty items, but the material quickly found more important applications in illuminated signs, lighting fixtures, windows, and streamlined lenses for automobile taillights. As the product evolved, it found more sophisticated uses in contact lenses, optical fibers, and dentures. Plastic lenses proved far lighter and were more resistant to breaking than glass. They could also be manufactured with greater precision and in a wider variety of streamlined shapes. In time, the Plexiglas® in automobile headlamps and other light lenses was largely replaced by polycarbonates. Continuous advances in plastics technology were increasingly embraced by a once leery public, but no new synthetic polymer created the same furor as nylon.

Eight days after World War II ended, DuPont resumed production of nylon for consumer use and nearly began World War III on the streets of America. As Jeffrey Meikle wrote, "Nylons—or rather their lack—so directly symbolized wartime sacrifices of Americans on the home front, especially those of women, that they rushed to acquire stockings as tangible evidence of the nation's return to normalcy."

When the first of the newly made nylons went on sale, department stores became virtual battlegrounds. What came to be known as the Nylon Riots took place in cities across the United States. On February 6, 1946, Macy's, "the world's largest store," took out an advertisement in *The New York Times*. "Yesterday Macy's sold 50,000 pairs of nylons," the ad opened, "an apology to those who didn't get theirs. To them we want to say that we're terribly sorry. We'll be selling nylons again. We wish we could tell you when or how, but we don't know ourselves. Please continue to be patient with us." Fistfights broke out among customers, and scuffles with police officers were common occurrences. In Pittsburgh, 40,000 people fought over 13,000 pairs of available nylons. The local newspaper headline read: WOMEN RISK LIFE AND LIMB IN BITTER BATTLE OVER NYLONS. Within a year, further threats of violence and conflict in American department stores were averted as DuPont's production of nylon finally met the surging consumer demand.

Stockings being just one use of the innovative fiber, the physical properties of nylon led to its incorporation in other consumer items, including carpeting and automobile upholstery. Nylon was strong, resistant to abrasion and chemicals, and low in moisture absorbency. Dresses, outerwear, windbreakers, and bedspreads made with nylon were embraced by consumers. Its flexibility and strength led to improved versions of conveyer and seat belts, tennis racket strings, and sleeping bags. There was no stopping the advance of plastics into people's daily lives.

Some beginnings, however, can be difficult. Before the war there were few synthetic products; after 1945 the polymer floodgates opened. At first, nylon stockings being a notable exception, consumers did not openly welcome other synthetic products. Their early experiences with plastic products proved less than convincing. While scientists built on knowledge gained during the war and experimented with new formulas and molding techniques, inexperienced new manufacturers, including former soldiers with access to surplus war plastics, became overnight manufacturers. They produced flimsy toys, doodads, and novelty items. These products, according to Penny Sparke, "left the consumer thinking them only

PLASTIC'S ABILITY TO BE MOLDED, COUPLED WITH THE DIVERSE CHARACTERISTICS OF INDIVIDUAL PLASTICS, LEAD TO THE CREATION OF INNOVATIVE PRODUCTS THAT ARE BOTH FUNCTIONAL AND STYLISH.

cheap-looking, unreliable and short-lived." Products often failed because the novice manufacturers chose improper resins. Most people at the time thought all plastics were interchangeable and did not realize that each individual plastic had its own strengths and weaknesses. The plastics industry realized the serious implications of these erroneous assumptions and focused their second National Plastics Exposition in 1947 on choosing "the right plastic for the right purpose."

It was an era in which large corporations such as DuPont and General Electric coexisted with self-taught experimenters, inventors, and opportunists, all seeking a place in the plastics industry. Alan Vivat was a young man who sold finished plastic products door to door in post–World War II Boston. The products he carried were manufactured by a small company that employed women to cut and sew the items in their homes from rolls of clear plastic obtained from large plastics producers. He sold tablecloths, appliance and furniture covers, shower caps, and aprons. "It was so new," he reminisced, "people didn't know anything about plastic. But when they realized that it can protect their clothes, oh boy!"

It was only a matter of time before the industry went from producing durable plastic coverings to developing new fabrics that made life easier for consumers. In the early 1950s DuPont went a step beyond plastic sheeting to change American fashions as well. Orlon®, an acrylic that in many ways duplicated the look and plush feel of natural wool, provided a "wash and wear" capability that soon made it a popular fabric for carpets, sweaters, stuffed animals, and imitation fleece. Unlike wool, acrylic garments retained their shape, dried quickly, and were resistant to moths.

The 1950s also introduced Fiber V, a polyester material that DuPont called Dacron®. It revolutionized the clothing industry and became the most widely used synthetic fiber in the world. A 1952 newspaper advertisement for men's suits made of Dacron® exclaimed, "Surprisingly rugged. Will outlast many a sizzling summer! Yet, for all its strength, 'Dorian Spun' is s-m-o-o-t-h and soft, porous and light in weight. More— it is not prone to wrinkles. The few that appear during the day generally hang out overnight."

Polyester was developed and patented in England in 1943 but licensed to DuPont and other fiber producers around the world. Dacron® and other polyesters became popular fibers for men's suits. Not only were the new suits machine washable, they also could be drip-dried without losing their shape or crease. The "wash and wear" family of synthetic fabrics forever changed people's dress habits. With the increased availability of washing machines and dryers, people found themselves freed from the often grueling washday chores of scrubbing and ironing. Synthetic fibers offered consumers flexibility and variety as the fabrics could be used alone or to enhance natural fibers such as wool and cotton. By the end of the 1950s most of the twentieth century's basic synthetic fibers had been developed. Scientists then began working with the existing fibers to develop more innovative uses and achieve more complex refinements.

Top fashion designers today use natural and synthetic fibers interchangeably. The synthetics are popular because they duplicate the feel and look of natural fibers while providing easy maintenance. Look down at your feet. You probably are wearing footwear made in part of a plastic. Lightweight, moldable into any desired shape, the bottoms of our shoes and sneakers are flexible yet firm, skid resistant and shock absorbent. Shoe inserts are light and soft and give wearers a comfortable fit making the shoes last longer while being resistant to moisture and microbes.

Some synthetic fibers have become indispensable particularly for astronauts, soldiers, police officers, and firefighters because of unique safety features. Aramid and PBI were new fibers that went beyond the "drip and dry" promises to form garments that were highly flame resistant and able to maintain shape at high temperatures. These innovative fibers were used to make firefighters' protective clothing, helmets, and vests. Another fiber, Kevlar®, was invented by DuPont scientists Stephanie Kwolek and Herbert Blades in 1966 and immediately began saving the lives of police officers because of its ability to protect them from gunshots. Kevlar® is lightweight, rustproof, and five times stronger

SPECIALLY TREATED FABRICS PROVIDE FIREPROOF PROTECTION FOR FIREFIGHTERS AND OTHER PUBLIC SAFETY PERSONNEL.

than the same weight of steel. Bullet-resistant vests are now virtually required wear for police officers. Kevlar® has other applications, too, and is used to make fiber-optic cables, train and automobile brakes, mooring ropes, and canoes.

Jeffrey Meikle writes that after World War II, "dominance in the plastic industry shifted from thermosets to such thermoplastics as polyethylene— garbage pails, squeeze bottles, hula hoops—flexible, lighter and less permanent." By the beginning of the twenty-first century, more than 70 percent of the fiber used around the world was manufactured. Plastics had dramatically changed the way people live and play.

Plastics are in nearly everything from golf balls to trash bags, from food containers to computers. Newer plastic forms have allowed manufacturers to expand into areas previously limited to natural materials. Zippers, previously made of metal, became plastic; glass bottles gave way to plastic ones. By the late 1970s plastic milk, juice, and soda containers had all but replaced the glass originals. Consumers found the new bottles safer and resistant to breakage. Over time, the weight of empty plastic soda bottles has dropped 25 percent, while 1-gallon (3.8-liter) plastic milk jugs now weigh 30 percent less than they did twenty years ago. Ketchup and mustard became even easier to dispense with the invention of squeezable plastic bottles. In 2001 the classic Gerber single-serving glass baby-food jars were replaced, for some of its offerings, by shatterproof plastic containers that provided the same level of purity.

In the early 1950s polyethylene was the most widely used plastic. It was shatterproof, moisture proof, and flexible at low temperatures, making it perfect for such diverse products as golf balls and ice cube trays. In hospitals and doctors' offices, it appeared in the form of the tubing and sheeting used in surgical procedures. Within years, it was the popular choice of food manufacturers to package fresh and frozen vegetables. Other polymers were equally as versatile and brought changes of their own.

Polystyrene was used to make ice buckets, laundry baskets, and refrigerator drawers. A later version, polypropylene, was more durable and used in milk crates, toilet seats, tables, chairs, and appliance cases. In its best known form as foamed polystyrene, usually referred to by its trade name, Styrofoam®, it is used as flotation devices, picnic coolers, egg cartons, fast-food restaurant containers, and those annoying packing "peanuts." The food industry relied on polystyrene packaging because it was strong but lightweight, provided excellent insulation, and since it was also disposable, created a sanitary way of presenting food. In its solid form, polystyrene is used to make plastic cutlery, yogurt cups, and CD and DVD holders, or jewel boxes. ABS, a co-polymer of acrylonitrile, butadiene, and styrene, was used to mold one-piece liners for refrigerators. As molded nylon, it was fashioned into long-lasting self-lubricating gears and bearings.

THEY MAY SOMETIMES BE A NUISANCE, BUT PACKING PEANUTS AND OTHER PACKAGING MATERIALS KEEP ITEMS SAFE AND INTACT DURING SHIPPING.

The modern automobile industry currently uses one-twentieth of all plastics produced. Nearly every part of today's automobiles, from bumpers to door panels, contains a form of plastic. Plastics allow engineers greater freedom in styling, constructing, and placing components. Unlike metal, automobile bodies made of plastic are more resistant to dents, and because they are lighter, they provide drivers with higher gas mileage. The modern automobile contains about 14 percent plastic by weight. Because plastic is lighter than steel, the total number of plastic parts is much greater than those made of other materials. Unfortunately, when a car is scrapped, most of the plastics cannot be reused.

Plastic is the material of choice for automobile interiors, appearing as the side trim, knobs and displays, door handles, heating and cooling vents, speaker grills, and even cup holders. The instrument panel, with its dials and see-through protective coverings, is made up of a number of plastics. Under the hood, a car could not run without plastic parts, including fan blades, radiator hoses, and antifreeze containers. Plastic fuel tanks, oil pans, and nylon fuel lines are resistant to chemical degradation, and water pumps, previously prone to rust, are now fabricated with plastics.

After the war, a number of veterans created consumer uses for fiberglass, a material they had come to appreciate for its wartime uses. Fiberglass had special properties as an insulator that combined the strength of glass with the flexibility of plastic resin. The material was not complicated to use but was labor intensive to mold. It was fashioned into surfboards and the bodies of streamlined sports cars and dune buggies. For do-it-yourself hobbyists, fiberglass was the perfect material to create their own sports car bodies which were dent proof, squeak proof, and lightweight. In 1953 General Motors released the two-seated Chevrolet Corvette, the first mass-produced car with a fiberglass body. Fiberglass allowed the car's designers to create a sculptured design. Boat manufacturers benefited as well, designing crafts that were streamlined, would not corrode in water, and were easy to shape. Other companies used fiberglass to design chairs with modern shapes.

THE 1953 CHEVROLET CORVETTE WAS THE FIRST CONSUMER AUTOMOBILE WITH AN ALL-FIBERGLASS BODY.

Many modern uses of plastic material developed accidentally or as a direct result of the curiosity of scientists. In 1948 a Swiss engineer, George de Mestral, went for a hike. When he came home he found burrs stuck to his clothes. They were firmly attached and difficult to dislodge. Sensing that the idea behind this naturally occurring nuisance could have consumer appeal in the form of a closing or fastening device, he set to work. Eight years later he perfected a synthetic hook-and-loop system that duplicated nature. He called his discovery Velcro® hook-and-loop fasteners. The "hook tape" had stiff synthetic barbs on it while the "loop tape" was soft and fuzzy. Together they formed a loose yet firm bond that to this day helps kids keep their shoes on and their jackets closed.

In the late 1940s and during the 1950s, a few individuals greatly advanced the image of plastics. Perhaps the most visible was Earl Tupper who dabbled in several failed businesses before starting work in 1937 as a sample maker at DuPont's Doyle Works plastic plant in Leominster, Massachusetts. Even as a child, he had considered himself an inventor and tinkered with a number of creative ideas. After two years of familiarizing himself with the techniques and processes of plastic manufacturing, he bought some molding equipment and started a company of his own, Tupper Plastics, which produced plastic containers and beads. All the while he continued tinkering with molds and materials.

In 1945, as prices of raw plastic materials declined after World War II, DuPont provided samples of its flexible and lightweight polyethylene polymer to plastics manufacturers to encourage them to develop more products for consumer use. A problem with the product was its tendency to split. Tupper experimented and perfected DuPont's product and patented what he called Poly-T: Material of the Future, a refined form of polyethylene that could be colored and shaped into any form. His first manufactured product was a 7-ounce (198-gram) milky-white container that was nontoxic and unbreakable—the world's first piece of Tupperware. To circumvent the often negative image the public had of plastic, he called his products Poly-T. They were not only practical and affordable but beautifully designed. A 1947 article in *House Beautiful* heralded "Fine Art for 39 Cents." In 1956 articles of Tupperware were displayed at New York's Museum of Modern Art as symbols of the flair and practicality that characterized the new plastics age. Although Tupperware won awards for design, at first it was not a commercial success.

In 1947 Tupper had perfected his unique seals, which created a partial vacuum and made his plastic containers air and liquid tight, and so applied for a patent. But Tupper's seals had to fit the containers so precisely people had to be taught how to put them on to achieve the unique "burping" effect, which guaranteed no leakage would occur. Department store sales were slow, and Tupperware, despite its quality, might have disappeared from the market had it not been for the foresight of an entrepreneurial woman from Detroit named Brownie Wise.

A WOMAN HOLDS THREE TUPPERWARE CONTAINERS WHILE STANDING IN FRONT OF A GROUP GATHERED IN A LIVING ROOM FOR THE NOW FAMOUS TUPPERWARE PARTY. SOME OF THE WOMEN WEAR HATS MADE FROM THE PLASTIC CONTAINERS.

In 1951 Wise met with Tupper and Ann and Tom Damigella of Boston to discuss a special way of promoting Tupperware—the house party. She and the Damigellas had successfully been selling other products using the house party technique and believed they could do the same with Tupperware. They realized that nothing could replace a hands-on demonstration of how the Tupperware cover fit. Their sales targets were suburban housewives who tended to go food shopping less often than before the war thanks to the advent of larger refrigerators. An article in *U.S. News and World Report* explained, "The Tupperware party was one of the first new rituals in suburban America. Families were displaced and women, confined to their homes and children, felt the loss of adult companionship. Tupperware parties helped fill the void." While shoppers were concerned with keeping food fresh for as long as possible, after the hardships of World War II, they also generally looked for ways to make modern style and flair an integral part of their lives.

The sales force Wise envisioned was largely female. At a time when most women did not work outside the home, becoming a Tupperware demonstrator provided a job opportunity and exposure to the business world. The house parties sold Tupperware products but perhaps just as important to attendees, they became fun social events. By 1951 Tupper removed his products from store shelves and had them distributed exclusively through these innovative home parties. Wise soon became the public representative of the company since Earl Tupper shied away from publicity. She became the best known female business personality of her time. Stories about her appeared in national magazines. In 1958 she delivered a speech, "Ours Is a Woman's World," before the largely male National Association of Direct Selling Companies.

Another highly visible pattern of plastics use emerged in the toy industry. In the years before and shortly after World War II, cheaply constructed and quickly discarded plastic toys flooded the marketplace. Then, as Tupperware was helping to dramatically change plastic's image, a small toy company in California began creating plastic-based products that became internationally famous. Just as the modern plastics industry itself resulted from a combination of science and luck, the fun-loving founders of the Wham-O™ Company perfected toys that have captured the imagination of children all over the world and stood the test of time.

College students have always enjoyed hanging out together in their free time. Many students in the New England area also enjoyed the delicious pies made by the Frisbie Baking Company. When the students finished eating, they got into the habit of tossing the empty metal pie tins to one another on the campus lawns. In 1948 a California building inspector, Walter Morrison, and his business partner, Warren Franscioni, invented a plastic version of the original Frisbie tin that traveled farther and with greater accuracy than the original. They sold the rights to their "Pluto Platter" to the Wham-O™ Company, which modified the original design, changed its name to Frisbee®, in honor of the pie company, and began manufacturing the new disk in 1957. The rest is history.

The popularity of the Frisbee® became legendary and even led to the development of an organized sport, ultimate Frisbee®. But it was another Wham-O™ product that became an even greater international fad. Arthur Melin and Richard Knerr, the company's founders, discovered that Australian children enjoyed playing with bamboo hoops during their

FRISBEES HAVE BECOME POPULAR TOYS FOR YOUNG AND OLD ALIKE. THEY ARE ONE OF THE MOST FAMILIAR AND POPULAR PLASTIC TOYS EVER MADE.

physical education classes. Wham- O™ produced a polyethylene version which they called the hula hoop. Made of a material that was easy to form, it was safer for children to use compared to toys constructed of metal or wood. Again, as with Tupperware, the marketing of the hula hoop was the crucial ingredient to its success.

At first, Melin took his plastic hula hoop to neighborhood playgrounds to demonstrate its use. As the toy grew in popularity, he hired skilled demonstrators to appear in toy and department stores around the country. The results were amazing. By the end of 1959, one hundred million hoops had been sold as the fad spread throughout the world. So much polyethylene was used to meet demand for the toy that shortages of the plastic began to affect its other uses, particularly in construction.

Another popular toy had its origins in serious science. In 1943 Jim Wright, a General Electric engineer, was working on the development of synthetic rubber. In one of his experiments, he mixed silicone oil and boric acid and produced a rubberlike material that puzzled him. The elastic material bounced, withstood fluctuations in temperature, and was resistant to rot but did not seem to have any practical applications. General Electric sent samples out to other engineers to see if they could figure out what to do with it. The engineers had fun with it but could not come up with a pragmatic use. One of their clever discoveries was that, once pressed onto a newspaper or comic book, the rubbery material took on the image of the printing or illustration which could then be manipulated and stretched.

In 1950 a New Haven, Connecticut, toy store owner, Ruth Fallgatter, bought a ton of the seemingly useless material from General Electric for $147. She formed the puttylike substance into small 1-ounce (28-gram) balls which she packed into brightly colored plastic eggs. Silly Putty® was an instant hit—at first with adults. But it did not take long for children to discover it. Since 1950, more than 300 million eggs of Silly Putty® have been sold around the world.

Even older toy favorites could not escape the plastic revolution. Dolls became increasingly formed of plastic as were new incarnations such as

Hasbro's G.I. Joe® and Mr. Potato Head® and Mattel's ever-popular Barbie®. Even the steel Slinky® spring toy, invented in 1943 by Richard James, began to be manufactured in plastic in 1978. "We decided to make Slinkys® in plastic," Betty James, the company's president said, "because younger children tangled the metal ones too easily and had trouble holding onto them. With plastic, we can manufacture a larger diameter Slinky® which is easier for small hands to manage and we can produce it in bright colors that really appeal to children." Slinkys®, hula hoops, Frisbees®, and Silly Putty® outlived the faddish phase of their existence and remain popular toys and amusements today.

A fad of a different kind was set off in 1957 when Don Featherstone, a young designer at Union Products in Leominster,

THE PLASTIC HULA HOOP CONTINUES TO BE A FAVORITE TOY AROUND THE WORLD. HERE, A TALENTED GIRL BREAKS THE WORLD RECORD FOR HULA-HOOP TWIRLING IN 1958, NOT ALLOWING EVEN A SNACK BREAK TO INTERRUPT HER WINNING EFFORT.

Massachusetts, created the plastic pink flamingo. In the 1950s the growth of the suburbs forever changed American life. A key part of suburban life centered on the lawn. Great expenditures of money and labor went toward the upkeep of the carefully groomed outdoor spaces. Lawn ornaments were one way for home owners to personalize the look of their property. No ornament reached the popularity of the pink plastic bird created by Don Featherstone, who referred to his creation as "affordable bad taste accessible to the American masses." Soon plastic flamingos were everywhere. Since 1957 twenty million pairs of the pink flamingos have been sold around the world creating a subculture of fans who find the plastic birds endearing if not just a bit hokey.

Tupperware and hula hoops, despite their commercial success and visibility, played only a small role in the increase of plastics use in the 1950s and 1960s. It was a period that saw not only the increasing availability of new materials and products but of lifestyle change as well. Early consumers rarely understood the differences among the various materials and were only beginning to get used to the notion of plastics. As early as 1947, *House Beautiful,* a magazine geared to women, devoted a special issue to "Plastics. A Way to a Better More Carefree Life." It stressed the easy upkeep of plastic products and "damp-cloth cleaning." In 1953 another women's magazine, *McCalls,* offered an educational booklet to readers, "Plastics: Everything a Woman Could Ask For," which taught, "The greatest asset of plastics is their difference, so you can select the right one for the job."

The booklet described the major plastics then available and the specific products made from each that could be used in a home. The list was quite impressive:

Acrylics *(Lucite®, Plexiglas®)*
Salad bowls, picture frames, trays, lamp bases

Phenolics *(Bakelite, Catalin, Marblette)*
Radio and television cabinets, cutlery handles, electrical parts

Urea *(Beetle, Plaskon)*
Buttons, jar tops, picnic ware

Melamine *(Melmac)*
Dinnerware, mixing bowls, hearing aid cases

Cellulosics *(Pyralin, Tenite)*
Lamp shades, toys, household tool handles

Polyethylene *(Alathon)*
Ice cube trays, spray bottles, bathroom cups, waste baskets

Polystyrene *(Styron, Styrofoam®)*
Storage bowls, tumblers, kitchen ware

Vinyls *(Dow PVC, Velon, Pliovic)*
Shower curtains, garment bags, floor and wall tiles, garden hose

Saran *(Saran®, Velon)*
Rugs, wraps, insect screens, upholstery, drapery fabrics

Even as plastic consumer items began filling American homes, the industry was looking to the future. Between 1957 and 1967, 20 million visitors to Disneyland marveled at one of the theme park's most popular attractions, the Monsanto House of the Future, a dwelling made almost entirely of plastic. It was designed to give visitors a look into the future—1987. Three years in the planning at the Massachusetts Institute of Technology, the house was a collaboration between the plastics industry and designers. The shell of the house was composed of a series of U-shaped sections of reinforced fiberglass panels laid on their sides to

VISITORS TO DISNEYLAND IN 1957 TOUR THE ALL-PLASTIC MONSANTO HOUSE OF THE FUTURE.

form the ceiling, floor, and walls of a streamlined room. Each of the four rooms was supported by beams that cantilevered from a central core to support the structure. Ten years after the house had been built, when the exhibit closed, contractors had a difficult time tearing down the plastic walls. The structure was so solid, neither jackhammers, steel wrecking balls, nor chain saws could penetrate the dwelling. It finally had to be broken into pieces small enough to cart away.

While the architecture was eye-catching and an indication of the strength and versatility plastics could lend to home construction, it was the interior demonstrations of plastic-based appliances and furnishings that captured the attention of visitors. Rugs and upholstery coverings were made of synthetic fibers. Even the models who posed for pictures wore clothes made of synthetic fibers. Easy-to-clean laminates, such as Formica® which could be manufactured in a wide range of colors and designs, were used on the cabinets, counters, and wall surfaces. Molded plastic chairs surrounded a plastic table topped with plastic dishes. In the bathroom, the tub, shower, and sink were made of reinforced plastic. The latest in audiovisual equipment, radios, televisions, a record player, and a push-button telephone were also molded of plastic.

Although highlighting the role plastics could play in home building and furnishing, the popularity of the Disneyland prototype did not translate into a rush to construct similar houses for actual families. (The House of the Future was not the only plastic building at Disneyland. Sleeping Beauty's own castle was constructed in part of fiberglass-reinforced plastic.) Despite its futuristic design, which today may seem old fashioned, some of the innovations introduced in the Monsanto house have become standard practice in modern construction. Houses today contain plumbing, insulation, countertops, and showers made of plastic. Plastics in furniture have also become commonplace whether as an imitation of classic wooden items or as a material in its own right. By the 1970s expensive one-of-a-kind artist-designed plastic tables and chairs had given way to similarly stylish mass-produced items, priced to fit the budgets of most families.

With the dawn of the space age in the last half of the twentieth century, plastics made previously unthought-of applications possible, not only helping to send people into space but leading to the proliferation of new products and material on earth. Without plastics, space exploration would not have been a reality. Lightweight plastics were used to fashion fuel tanks and the external parts of space vehicles, and to provide insulation. Other plastics were used to build solar cells to generate power. Inside the manned space vehicles, astronauts were outfitted in multilayered polymer spacesuits that protected them from high temperatures yet allowed a great deal of flexibility. Polymer-constructed air-quality sensors and life-support systems within the cabins kept the astro-

WITHOUT PLASTICS, SPACE EXPLORATION WOULD NOT BE POSSIBLE.

nauts safe. On July 20, 1969, Neil Armstrong planted an American flag on the moon. It was made of nylon.

From the science of space travel evolved common products that are taken for granted today. The insulated bags used to deliver pizza contain heat reflectors based on the metallized polymer films used to protect astronauts. Plastic video game joysticks are modeled on specialized hand controllers used to steer space shuttle modules. Drawing from space suit designs, ski boots today are more flexible. Life-support systems worn by astronauts have been used as models for lightweight breathing systems employed by firefighters, coal miners, and rescue teams.

Music lovers have also counted themselves among the beneficiaries of plastic development. Early recordings were on disks made of shellac, a natural polymer. The black 78-revolutions-per-minute (rpm) record was standard until after World War II. In 1946 the 12-inch (30-centimeter) transparent Vinylite Red Seal record playing disk was created with narrower grooves that could be played back at a slower speed (45 rpm). In 1948 Peter Goldmark, an engineer at CBS, developed the long playing 33⅓ rpm record. This vinyl disk gave a record 250 grooves versus the 80 grooves on the traditional 78 rpm shellac recording. The 1940s also saw the development of audio tape, vinyl acetate film coated with tiny metal particles. Reel-to-reel tape gave way to cassette audiotape and then to CDs and DVDs. None of this would have been possible without plastics.

Computer technology has also been transformed by the use of plastics to create the housing and protective shells for monitors and central processing units (CPUs) and to shrink electronic components. The iPod® and the cellular telephone are good examples of how plastics have been able to accommodate dramatic miniaturization of electronics.

Plastics have even transformed the way sports are played. In the United States, major league baseball uniforms are made of 100 percent polyester, while major league basketball uniforms are made of nylon. In addition, professional sports leagues require players to wear synthetic socks for health and safety.

Specialized plastics can be found used in many sports today in a variety of ways. Properties such as impact absorption, slippage and weather resistance, strength, and durability have led to plastics replacing previously used natural materials such as wood. In tennis racquets, for example, nylon, Kevlar®, and polyester have largely replaced natural fibers made from animal intestines. Synthetic strings do not break as often and provide variable tension that can be adjusted to fit an individual's expertise. Today's tennis racquet handles have better grips that resist rain or perspiration. Tennis balls are formed around hollow cores of inflated rubber.

On the water, the bodies of sailboats as well as their sails are usually constructed of plastics. Fiberglass or laminates are used to provide hull stability and boat interiors. Sails made of plastic fibers such as polyester offer strength while retaining their shape. Canoeing enthusiasts today use plastic paddles to direct their plastic vessels. Unlike wood, plastic does not warp and can withstand extreme environmental conditions. Other recreational boats are largely made of plastics, especially fiberglass coated with urethane or polyester, which helps keep the original color from fading.

But perhaps the greatest contribution plastics have made to the sports world is in the area of safety. Gymnasts perform on floor mats made of several layers of protective plastics including polyethylene or vinyl-covered polyurethane foam, which absorbs shock from hard landings. Vaulting horses and balance beams have vinyl covers and foam fillers, which allows for better grip and moisture absorption than wood and also prevents serious head injuries. In baseball, plastics are key components of batting helmets, catcher's equipment, and even "breakaway" bases. Catchers, for example, are subject to high-risk impact from balls thrown at more than 95 miles (153 kilometers) per hour. They are protected by face masks made of metal coated with plastics and padded with imitation leather to protect their eyes, nose, and throat. Plastic chest protectors are also worn to guard the body. Soccer players wear plastic shin guards to sheathe their legs and plastic gloves to let them securely grip the ball, in which polyurethane has largely replaced traditional leather. One soccer ball manufacturer explained, "Polyurethane has a longer life and can take more beatings without going out of shape." For outdoor enthusiasts, polyurethane-coated rain and sailing jackets and ski suits keep out the wet and cold, while keeping the wearer warm and dry. Modern-day skis, snowboards, and wakeboards all have polyurethane cores, ensuring they are lightweight and strong, even at low temperatures.

THE INNER SURFACE OF THE NYLON FABRIC OUTER SHELL IS COATED WITH POLY-
URETHANE. THE COATING MAKES THE FABRIC WATERPROOF YET ALLOWS IT TO "BREATHE."
FABRICS WITH THIS TYPE OF COATING ARE HIGHLY RESISTANT TO TEARING AND ABRASION.

Another use of polymers is in the development of a variety of adhesives that have become integral to everyday products. One estimate is that the average automobile has more than 20 pounds (9 kilograms) of adhesives that are used to hold its various plastic parts together. Other plastic-based adhesives are used in such wide-ranging products as tapes, labels, bandages, and tooth implants.

Teflon®, Roy Plunkett's accidental discovery, grew from a World War II wonder material to a modern kitchen convenience as a coating for cookware. As the slipperiest synthetic polymer, its nonstick properties and ability to withstand high heat have led to its use in other forms. Ice skaters no longer have to wait for cold weather; they can just as easily practice on Teflon®-coated surfaces in the middle of the summer. Automobile bolts coated with Teflon® result in rattle-free rides. Teflon® resins are used in fabricating space suits, heat shields, and insulation. Teflon® fibers are employed to make friction-free socks, which help reduce skin irritation for people with diabetes. As a protector in liquid form, Teflon® repels water and other stains from clothing, carpeting, and even the Statue of Liberty.

Paper or plastic? Plastics have revolutionized the food industry. The first plastic sandwich bags were introduced in 1957. Today innovative packaging materials continue to keep foods fresh while the plastic bags in which the food is carried home are lighter and cheaper than paper. Plastic bags require less energy to produce than paper bags and conserve fuel in shipping. By 2000 four out of five grocery bags were made of plastic.

In so many ways, whether visible as plastic packaging or embedded within electronic devices, plastics have forever changed the way we live our lives. Plastic parts and insulation in refrigerators and air conditioners have improved energy efficiency and make the appliances run more quietly than earlier models. Think about the microwave oven. Not only are plastics a visible part of microwave cases and liners, but without the variety of plastic containers in which to heat up food, using a microwave would be quite messy. Food manufacturers are increasingly turning from metal packaging to plastic to provide consumers with conveniences such as the ability to heat, reheat, and store a variety of packaged foods from complete dinners to soups and desserts. Getting food to market, particularly fresh fruits, vegetables, and meat, has become easier and safer because of plastics. Today, as perishable food travels long distances from the farm to our homes, it is transported in refrigerated containers and vehicles constructed from metal-faced "sandwich" panels insulated with a core of polyurethane foam. Once in our homes, the food continues to be protected by the same polyurethane foam that insulates our refrigerators.

Can you imagine your world without plastics?

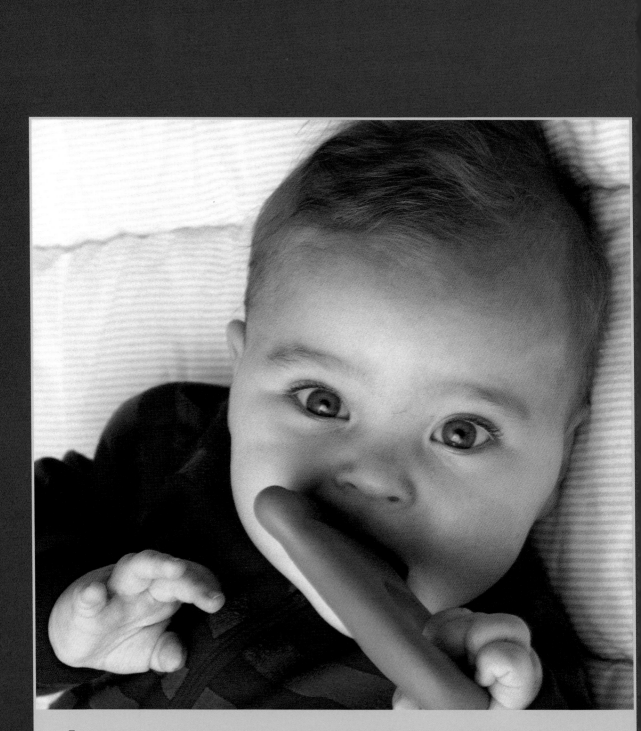

FROM TEETHING RINGS TO FORMULA BOTTLES, PLASTICS BRING CONVENIENCE TO MODERN NURSERIES.

A Healthier World

"Increasingly, we are becoming creatures made of
flesh, bone and plastic."
—*Los Angeles Times*

Just as plastics have changed the way we live, they have
also dramatically affected life itself. Our lives are safer, longer, and more
productive because of medical advances made possible by the development of plastic devices, systems, and packaging. Compared to metal
and glass, items made of plastics cost less while still being sanitary and
disposable. They can be easily molded into shapes and configurations
that would be difficult to duplicate using glass and metals and thus making possible life-saving medical procedures that did not previously exist.
Plastics are safer than glass since they are shatterproof yet remain
clear, strong, and flexible. Often plastics, like glass, can also be resistant
to harsh disinfectants and sterilization procedures.

Plastics have become an indispensable part of our health, beginning
with the moment of birth. Premature babies have a much improved sur-
vival rate because of modern incubators made of clear plastic and Plexi-
glas®. Controlled heat within the air-filtered, humidified, and ventilated
incubator permits babies to thrive and survive.

The next time you hear an ambulance siren, think about the many
plastic-based products on board that stabilize patients on the way to
the hospital. Emergency technicians rely on inflatable splints, surgical
gloves, thermal blankets, and inhalation masks and tubing to keep patients stable. For accident victims, the use of hard plastic backboards,

and neck immobilization collars restrict patient movements that might cause even more damage to already injured bodies.

The familiar adhesive bandage we use to cover a scrape or cut has evolved into a life-saving form thanks to military necessity. A major cause of death in combat has been uncontrolled bleeding, with about 50 percent of those who died on the battlefield bleeding to death in minutes. Today, new blood-clotting plastic bandages save battlefield lives. Developed in cooperation with the U.S. Army and the American Red Cross, these bandages are coated with clotting proteins and permit a wounded soldier or comrade to temporarily stop a life-threatening wound while awaiting evacuation to a field hospital. Another military innovation is the one-handed tourniquet, which allows an isolated soldier to stop bleeding from an arm or leg without assistance. At the heart of the new tourniquet are loops of nylon webbing that tighten when pulled to shut off blood flow. These plastic-based items can withstand blunt force as well as inclement weather and variable temperatures.

Another innovation from military medicine now being perfected is the Plasti-Bone, a specially coated polymer "bone" that can be surgically implanted where a damaged bone has been removed. Ranji Vaidyanathan, inventor of the procedure, explained the process: "What is left of the real bone attaches itself to the polymer bone after about 8 weeks. Then, the real bone begins to 'grow through' the porous scaffold. As it does, it 'eats' the scaffold. . . . In eighteen months, the expectation is that the bone will grow back completely, leaving the patient with natural bone."

For people who have lost an eye due to injury or disease, it is a great comfort to know their loss is not obvious to others. Today prosthetic eyes are almost indistinguishable from real ones. Although some people still refer to them as "glass eyes," they are actually made from medical-grade acrylic. A highly trained ocularist uses a plastic disk which is painted to duplicate the color and texture of the patient's real eye.

As with other applications, the right plastic must be matched to its specific uses and purposes. Polyvinyl chloride (PVC) is used in about

25 percent of all medical plastics because of its low cost, wide range of applications, and the ease with which it is processed. It is used in the manufacture of tubing, catheters, blood bags, oxygen delivery systems, and packaging. Other plastics such as polypropylene and polystyrene are used whenever high transparency is needed. The strength and durability of polyethylene make it an ideal material for use in artificial hips, knees, and shoulder joints. Polycarbonates, combining rigidity and heat resistance, are used to make equipment cases and surgical instrument handles. Because of their high transparency, they are also

PLASTICS HAVE MADE THE ORIGINAL "GLASS EYES" LIGHTER AS WELL AS MORE COMFORTABLE AND REALISTIC LOOKING.

used to make eyeglass lenses and provide vision-impaired people with shatterproof and lightweight lenses. For those who wish, soft plastic contact lenses provide another means of improving sight.

Plastics have become the material of choice for medical device manufacturers, because the substances are lightweight and durable. Chemists continually experiment with plastics and plastics additives to create material that can be molded to smaller dimensions, without compromising its inherent strength, to meet new demands for the miniaturization of medical devices. Innovations in technology have resulted in devices such as glucose meters for people with diabetes who must frequently check their blood sugar levels. New meters are being made that are not only smaller but are long lasting, internally lubricated, and have "gripping" surfaces for easy handling.

One of the hallmarks of twentieth-century medicine was the development of the artificial heart. In 1982 the Jarvik-7 artificial heart was implanted in the body of a retired dentist, Barney Clark. His own heart was close to shutting down and the Jarvik-7, made largely of plastic and polyester tubing, kept him alive an additional 112 days. The pump in his chest was tethered to a refrigerator-sized console that limited his mobility. Today, artificial hearts, used mainly as a temporary means of keeping patients alive while awaiting heart transplants, are smaller and connected to portable battery packs. Patients recovering from the procedure are able to continue with their daily lives.

The technology of the artificial heart was complex, although the concept was simple. Turning the idea into a workable model would not have been possible without plastics. The Texas Heart Institute describes the Jarvik-7's two pumps as working much like the heart's ventricles. Each sphere-shaped polyurethane ventricle has a disklike mechanism that pushes the blood from the inlet valve to the outlet valve. The artificial heart is attached to the heart's natural atria by cuffs made of Dacron® felt. The tubes leading out of the ventricular air chambers are made of reinforced polyurethane tubing. Where they exit the skin, the lines are sheathed in velour-covered Silastic to ensure stability and encourage tissue growth.

Other heart-assist devices have been implanted into patients who would otherwise not have survived their ailments, even for a short period. Implanted defibrillators and pacemakers with internal plastic parts and external tubing have provided patients with security and protection allowing them to maintain a high quality of life.

Complicated surgeries would also not be possible without the use of flexible plastic tubing. Catheters—small tubes—come in many different sizes and shapes. Cardiologists use them to insert special equipment into the body to diagnose or treat heart problems. Other catheters are

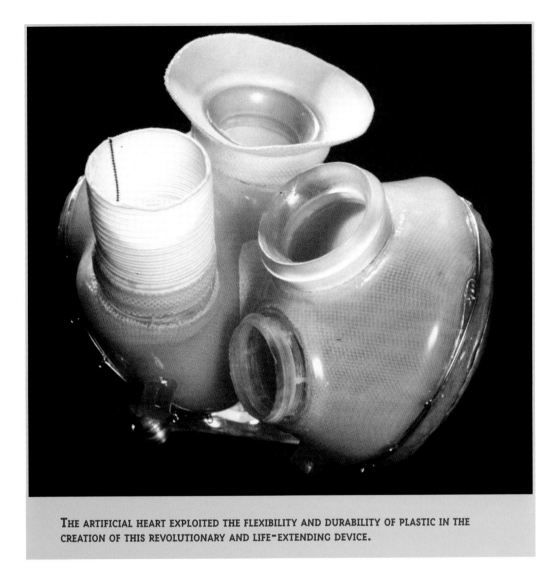

THE ARTIFICIAL HEART EXPLOITED THE FLEXIBILITY AND DURABILITY OF PLASTIC IN THE CREATION OF THIS REVOLUTIONARY AND LIFE-EXTENDING DEVICE.

used to extract fluids and to inject medicine into patient's veins. In turn, those fluids and medicines are contained in plastic bags. The earliest catheters were made from reeds, straws, and hollow leaves. The advent of flexible plastic tubing, replacing inflexible hollow metal or rubber tubes, meant that catheters could be used to save even more patients.

You do not have to undergo a heart transplant or invasive surgery, though, to experience the advances in medical care made possible by plastic. Ever skinned your knee? A plastic bandage covers the wound.

Visited the orthodontist lately? Chances are your braces contain plastic resulting in the lighter yet firm additions to your mouth. Want to prevent cavities? Dentists now paint thin plastic coatings on the chewing surfaces of your back teeth to prevent decay. The polymer sealants are slippery and make it harder for decay-causing plaque to stick to teeth. The sealants then form a barrier that protects pits and grooves against bacteria and food. If you do get a cavity, the filling used by the dentist will most likely also be made of plastic. And if you need a root canal to save a tooth, dentists today pack the tooth cavity with a flexible polymer filling that tightly molds and fills every tiny crevice and seals the tooth from further decay. The development of plastic even made a habit your dentist encourages—flossing—easier and more widely practiced. Prior to World War II, dental floss was not widely used. Made primarily from silk, the strands shredded easily. After the war, floss made from nylon or shredproof Teflon® became popularly accepted as a way of removing cavity-causing plaque from teeth.

Plastic in various forms also provides protection at the dentist's office. The dentist and hygienist may cover their faces with see-through plastic masks to protect themselves. The drill and x-ray equipment they use may have plastic covers as well on the handles to prevent cross-contamination to patients.

The low cost and flexibility of plastic products have made them indispensable in nearly all aspects of modern medicine and health care. At home, in doctor's offices, and in hospitals, seemingly every modern medical need or procedure revolves around plastic. Medicine cabinet drugs, whether prescription or over the counter, come in plastic bottles or jars. People with diabetes frequently test their blood with plastic meters. Asthmatics depend on their plastic inhalers.

Plastics not only serve as low-cost replacements for other materials but are used uniquely in their own right. A good example is in disk-replacement surgery. When adults complain of severe back pain, quite often it is a result of a spinal injury or degenerative disk disease. The deterioration of spinal disks affects the natural cushion that separates the spine's vertebrae. Until the middle of the twentieth century, corrective surgery was painful, complicated, and not necessarily successful. It often involved fusing disks with surgically implanted metal rods, which permitted vertebrae to grow together and bypass the injured disk. In October 2004 the Food and Drug Administration approved the marketing of the artificial disk, Charite, manufactured by the Johnson & Johnson Company. The disk, made of molecular-weight polyethylene placed between two metal plates, allows patients to move and bend naturally. Another system, developed by Disc Dynamics Incorporated, involves the insertion of an expandable polyurethane balloon injected with a polymer that specifically conforms to the shape and size of the space where the degenerated disk had been.

Because polyurethane can be formed into a variety of shapes, textures, and hardnesses, it can be used for other purposes in hospitals. It can be a solid or come in expanded, flexible, elastic, semirigid, or rigid forms. It is a favorite component of hospital pillows and mattresses because of its durability, ability to conform to a patient's shape or body configuration, and is suitable for patients who have asthma or allergies. In gel form, it is widely used as orthopedic shoe inserts and cushions. Because of polyurethane's ability to be molded and withstand heavy loads, it is also used to form the housings of dialysis machines, respiratory equipment, and light-therapy machines.

Medical institutions and hospitals are under constant pressure to lower costs while preserving quality. Disposable plastic laboratory flasks and dishes are packed in sterilized individual packages ensuring ease of use. Plastic packaging keeps medicine and surgical instruments sterile while specially engineered plastics make most of the sophisticated diagnostic and treatment technologies possible.

All medical providers are constantly monitoring the safety of the medications and treatments they prescribe for their patients. In hospitals, pharmacies, and doctor's offices, plastic packaging ensures proper individual dosages of medicines, particularly in liquid form. Before plastics, medicines were stored in glass bottles with ground glass stoppers which often became stuck in the bottles and were difficult to remove. Contrast that with today's functional plastic medicine bottles. Blister packs for pills and capsules make it easier to dispense medicines to patients while ensuring safety. This is particularly important with a growing population of older citizens who depend on medications and, in the case of diabetes, the self-injection of insulin at home.

Vials, syringes, and intravenous bags made of plastic allow physicians to eliminate contamination and protect themselves from being accidentally pricked with needles. Plastic syringes prefilled with exact doses of vaccines or medicines make it easier to efficiently inject large numbers of patients while eliminating contamination, misdosing, and the unnecessary waste of medicine. Plastic covers also protect the needles before and after use. Fear of contracting AIDS and other highly infectious diseases has made these plastic products indispensable by preventing cross-contamination for patients, health care workers, family members, and trash disposal workers.

Nowhere have medical plastics made such a visible impact as in the field of human engineering. Science-fiction films about the Bionic Man are not quite as far fetched as they may have once seemed. Today, engineers have created prosthetic devices of metal and plastics that provide increased mobility for growing numbers of people. Patients with broken or diseased hips or knees can now walk, dance, and lead otherwise normal lives—without pain—because of artificial joint replacements made possible by specially engineered plastics and metals.

For thousands of years, people whose hips had been worn down by arthritis or fractured because of an injury either lived in pain or became immobile. In the twentieth century, doctors began experimenting with surgical ways of repairing hips. They tried a variety of replacement material but nothing proved entirely effective until experiments with different plastic coatings yielded success. In 1958 Dr. John Charnley borrowed an acrylic bone cement from a dentist to firmly secure a polyethylene socket to the existing bone of a patient. Once in place, the polyethylene provided a tough and very slippery base that

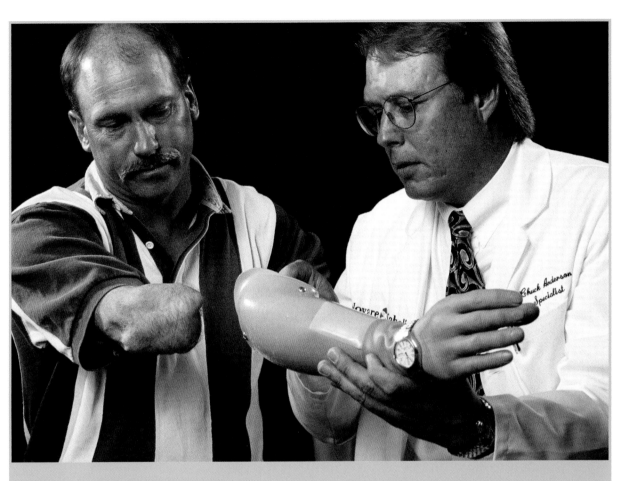

LIGHTWEIGHT, FLEXIBLE, AND REALISTIC LIMB REPLACEMENTS HAVE CHANGED THE WAY PROSTHETIC DEVICES ARE MADE.

allowed the artificial hip socket to move naturally and painlessly without friction. The total hip replacement operation was born. Since then, refinements in techniques and materials have made the operation an effective solution for hundreds of thousands throughout the world. In the 1970s similar advances were made in knee replacement surgery, again because of plastic components. Today, polymer screws, tacks, and nails help hold tissue in place while it reattaches to the bone. Eventually, these plastic fasteners melt away and disappear, allowing the load to transfer to the bone after healing is complete.

Modern medical plastics are being engineered to combat the biggest problem patients face with artificial prosthesis—infection. Researchers have developed ways of incorporating antibiotics and chemotherapy drugs into polyurethane. Today, some drugs can be targeted directly to the body part where they are needed because of biocompatible polymer systems that are used to encapsulate the drugs. An example is the use of biodegradable plastic implants to treat a form of brain cancer in which the drug-releasing implant wears away after the medicine is absorbed by the body.

Life-threatening blood clots during surgery can occur when foreign bodies such as tubing or catheters come in contact with blood. Today, new technology makes it possible to add anticlotting molecules to the vinyl used to make tubing and devices thereby decreasing the risk presented during critical life-saving procedures. Building on the same technology, scientists are working on a new "bionic" ear in which a polymer conducts electricity which then interacts with nerve cells to stimulate nerve growth. Other biodegradable plastics are being developed for use in surgical reconstruction, in which their unique structure delivers medicines that help spur the rapid growth of new and healthy cells and tissues.

Plastics have made our world safer, for people at all stages of life. Molded plastics allow such baby products as car seats, toys, and high chairs to have rounded corners which reduce the risk of contact injuries. Child-resistant medicine bottles are also tamperproof while shampoo bottles are shatterproof. Plastic sports safety gear including helmets, mouth guards, and knee pads keep players safe. Older people have benefited from vinyl bath mats, shower seats, and plastic pill bottles with markings. Everyone is safer because plastic is so prominently featured in automobiles, from safety belts to air bags to molded and contoured dashboards. Today, every automobile windshield in America has a built-in plastic liner that helps prevent dangerous shattering. Along with the role of plastics in promoting safety, today's automobiles contain fewer parts than those made just a few years ago, because of the ability to combine and assemble molded components.

Beyond medical uses, plastics have also changed the way we purchase and store our food. At the supermarket, fresh foods are protected from bacteria and spoilage by specialized plastic wrapping and packaging. Shoppers can clearly see what they are buying without worrying about whether the food has been touched or altered by others. Today's plastic packaging does more than protect food from handling but provides moisture barriers, resistance to flavor loss, and longer shelf life. A widely used technique, modified atmosphere packaging (known as MAP in the packaging industry), allows providers to pack fruits and vegetables, baked goods, and meat in atmosphere-controlled plastic bags that minimize the rate of product deterioration. The MAP process maintains the carbon dioxide/oxygen ratio at its optimum level, thus greatly extending the shelf life of the foods it protects. Bags of precut salad fixings would not be possible without this technology since lettuce, for example, begins to deteriorate almost immediately upon shredding. Tuna fish in vacuum-sealed plastic pouches has taken its place alongside traditional canned tuna on supermarket shelves. The pouches are not only easier to pack, they are lightweight, reclosable, and more convenient to store.

Foods with a longer shelf life can now be contained in a variety of both rigid and flexible packages, including several that rely on high-barrier properties to restrict oxygen exposure and flavor loss. These plastic containers, no matter what form they take, protect consumers from food-borne illnesses while keeping items protected against spoilage and contamination. They also provide convenience. One company won praise for its Italian dinners, flash-frozen and packed in metallized polyester pouches that can be microwaved in minutes. Another company makes a cake mix whose ingredients come with a polypropylene bowl. All the user has to do is empty the ingredient pouch into the bowl, add water, stir, and microwave. The bowl then becomes the serving dish: no muss, no fuss, as the advertising slogan goes.

Perhaps the best way of experiencing the changes plastics have made in the food industry is to walk the aisles of your neighborhood supermarket. From the MAP-sealed salads in the produce aisle to the

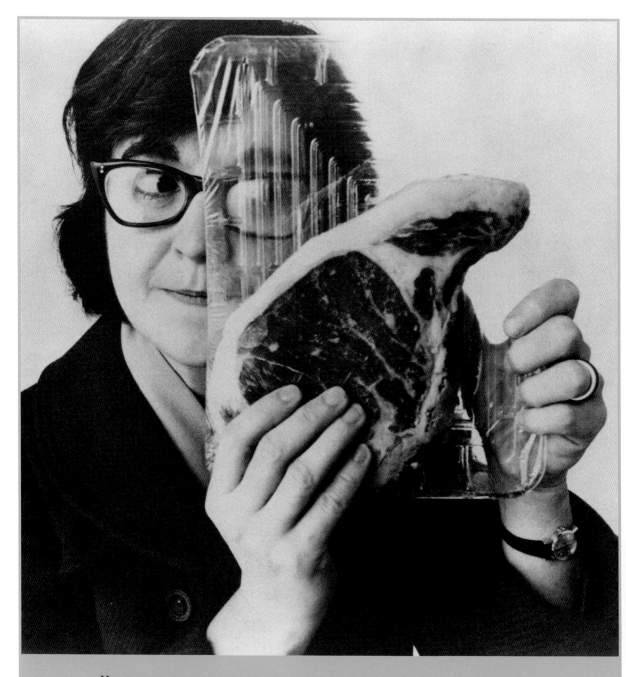

MODERN PACKAGING HAS BROUGHT CLEANLINESS TO CONSUMERS AND CHANGED THE WAY SHOPPERS BUY AND STORE THEIR FOOD PRODUCTS. AIRTIGHT CONTAINERS AND PLASTIC WRAP HELP KEEP FRESH FOOD SAFE AND ASSURE LONGER SHELF LIFE IN SUPERMARKETS.

carefully wrapped steaks in the meat department, the food is visible yet protected. Innovative plastic packaging brings us individual servings of chocolate pudding in the refrigerated section and tamperproof medicine bottles in the health and beauty aisles. We have come a long way from earlier times when open displays of meats and bulk dairy products predominated in local grocery stores.

The wide variety of plastics used in today's food industry ensures us all of convenience, safety, and purity. The plastic age has ushered in a cleaner, more sanitary era. Yet despite plastic's admirable attributes, innovation is often not without its problems. As the future of the planet is of growing concern, now more than ever, the negative impact of plastics threatens to overshadow the ways these revolutionary substances have benefited countless individuals.

AROUND THE WORLD, RECYCLING OFFERS A SOLUTION TO THE ENVIRONMENTAL EFFECTS OF EXCESS PLASTIC WASTE.

Plastics and the Environment

"... things to worry about from science ... genetic engineering,
transplanted heads, ... and the unrestrained growth of plastic flowers."
—Lewis Thomas

While there is much good news about the role of plastics in modern society, there is bad news as well. Since the beginning of the plastic age, concerns about the negative impact of these revolutionary materials on the environment and human health have clouded their many benefits. Most plastics are petroleum based but that is where the similarity among them ends. There are numerous production techniques and thousands of chemical additives, known as plasticizers, that are used to produce specific plastics to fit specific needs. To use polyvinyl chloride (PVC), for example, additives are used to produce a variety of thicknesses, characteristics, and degrees of solidity—from shower curtains to cables to tile flooring. Without these additives, PVC would not be usable.

Additives also play an important role in the medical uses of plastic. Phthalates are the ingredients that give polyvinyl chloride its flexibility and transparency. These characteristics result in the vinyl medical tubing that makes life-saving equipment, intravenous bags, and blood bags possible. Some health advocates have questioned the safety of phthalate in these medical products based on the negative effects the additive has displayed in experimental animals. Other plasticizers have provoked growing concerns about health dangers. An article in *Time* magazine explained, "Over time, according to a growing body of evidence, the chemicals that make up many plastics may migrate out of the material and into foods and fluids, ending up in your body." While the U.S. Food and Drug Administration (FDA) revealed that "the effects observed in animal studies could occur in humans," they added that "there are no human studies to date that show such effects." Nonetheless, doubts about the inherent safety of all plastics remain.

Concerns have not been limited exclusively to the chemical content of plastic products. In the 1950s and early 1960s, as the use of plastic bags became more widespread, several tragic incidents occurred as children accidentally suffocated when their faces became entangled in the plastic used by dry cleaners to cover and protect garments. Parents, unfamiliar with the danger involved, had tried to reuse plastic bags for other purposes. The otherwise useful coverings that kept clothes clean became known as "bags of death." The industry responded by imprinting notices on the bags ("This bag is not a toy," "Keep away from children—may cause suffocation."), warning parents to keep the coverings away from children. The plastics industry also began a successful public education campaign, which effectively curtailed the tragic deaths.

In the 1970s there were a series of tragic incidents involving sleepwear made of cotton and manufactured fibers, usually polyester, which caught fire easily and either killed or severely burned children. New laws were passed, and standards were set to assure that the fabrics used in making children's clothes were able to resist flames. Today, all children's clothing sold in the United States must be certified as flame retardant.

The same additives that give plastic products their valuable properties have also been targeted as dangerous to humans and the environment. Health advocates have long been concerned about the possible health risks of using plastics in cooking and food storage. They are concerned about chemicals that might leach into foods and beverages to create a health danger. Nearly all food-packaging materials contain substances that can migrate into the food they contact, including plasticizers used in food wrap. The FDA refers to these elements as food contact substances and must find them safe before they are permitted to be used. Additional concerns are raised by the complex manufacturing processes that create everyday plastic products. Air and water pollution can expose factory workers and nearby residents to toxic chemicals. Along with legitimate concerns, a number of myths about plastics—often incorrectly targeting phthalates—continue to circulate in newspapers and on Web sites.

One myth warns against the reuse of disposable water bottles, calling attention to what is identified as a cancer-causing element, DEHA, which is believed to be used to make polyethylene. Yet plastics manufacturers report that the polyethylene terephthalate (PET) used in water bottles does not contain DEHA. Another myth states that people should avoid using plastic food wraps and packages since they

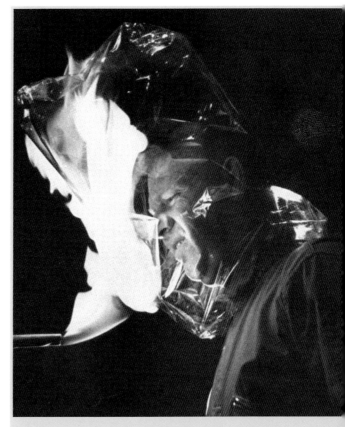

THIS GOVERNMENT OFFICIAL IS TESTING FIREPROOF PLASTIC FOR USE AS A SAFETY DEVICE IN THE EVENT OF A FIRE ON AN AIRPLANE. FLAME RESISTANCE AND RETARDANCE BECAME KEY CONCERNS IN THE CREATION OF PLASTIC-BASED PRODUCTS, ESPECIALLY IN SYNTHETIC FABRICS.

supposedly contain phthalates. Yet most plastic food packaging and storage items are made with PET, which is chemically different from polyvinyl chloride or its associated phthalates.

Rumors have been circulating for years warning against heating plastic containers in microwave ovens since a combination of fat, high heat, and plastics releases dioxin—a proven cancer-causing agent. The plastics industry contends that the claim is misleading, since dioxins are produced by combustion at temperatures typically greater than

700 degrees Fahrenheit (371 degrees Celsius), a temperature at which food would be so burned it would be inedible. Many of the plastics used to make today's wraps, packages, and containers are specially designed to withstand microwave temperatures. Dr. Edward Machuga of the FDA stated that the agency has "seen no evidence that plastic containers or films contain dioxins and knows of no reason why they would." On the other hand, the FDA advises consumers to make sure they are using specific plastic containers for their intended purposes and to always read directions on food packaging. Carryout containers from restaurants and margarine tubs, for example, should not be used in the microwave since inappropriate containers could melt or warp. Another recommendation is to place microwave-safe plastic wrap loosely over food and to allow space between the wrap and the food during heating.

In a classic race between competitors Coca-Cola and Pepsi-Cola to be the first to sell their carbonated beverages in plastic bottles, Coca-Cola won. In 1975 the Coca-Cola Company introduced its first plastic soda bottle, which had been developed by the Monsanto Chemical Company. However, before the bottles could ship, scientists discovered that the acrylonitrile material developed by Monsanto for the bottle could yield a trace amount of a suspected cancer-causing agent. The company notified the FDA, which banned the use of that plastic in food production.

Meanwhile, Pepsi had been experimenting with bottles made of another plastic, polyethylene terephthalate (PET), a material developed by the DuPont Company, which did not contain a suspect plasticizer. The PET bottle was designed by DuPont researcher Nathaniel Wyeth using a new technique involving stretching and blowing the plastic, a process called stretch-blow molding, which produced a bottle strong enough not to burst and safe enough to be accepted by the FDA. After the FDA banned acrylonitrile, Coca-Cola followed Pepsi's lead and used bottles made of PET. Since the introduction of the original plastic soft drink bottle, engineers have been able to shrink the amount of plastic used in the bottles, eliminating millions of pounds of packaging waste.

In 1958 the U.S. Congress passed the Food Additives Amendment to the existing Food, Drug and Cosmetic Act. The amendment contained the Delaney Clause, which states that no food additive shall be "deemed safe if it is found to induce cancer when ingested by man or animal." It set a rigid standard of zero tolerance. In 1996 the Delaney Clause was revised to allow for a "generally safe standard of reasonable certainty of no harm to consumers." In the 1950s it was thought that most human cancers were caused directly by chemicals. Today, it is understood that the major factors associated with cancer include tobacco use, dietary practices, and viruses. Yet chemicals are still related to health and environmental issues. Dioxins, as an example, are released into the air

THIS SODA BOTTLE FROM 1990 TRUMPS THE USE OF RECYCLED PLASTIC IN ITS CREATION. TODAY INCREASING AMOUNTS OF RECYCLED PLASTIC ARE BEING USED TO MANUFACTURE NEW ITEMS SUCH AS SODA BOTTLES AND OUTDOOR CLOTHING.

during the manufacture of chemicals and the burning of hazardous waste. They have been linked to cancer, birth defects, and weakened immune systems. They can travel over great distances, remain in the environment for long periods, and build up in the food chain.

Plastic toys, particularly for young children, have also come under attack. Vinyl has been a popular choice of toy manufacturers for its ability to be shaped in almost infinite ways to produce toys that can be either flexible or rigid. Again, it is the use of phthalates that gives PVC its flexibility. Environmental groups have argued that cancer-causing plasticizers can leach out of plastic toys and teething rings into the mouths of young children. The plastics industry has responded that the amount of such cancer-causing elements found in toys is small enough to have a negligible effect on children. Their view is echoed by the U.S. Consumer Product Safety Commission which stated "that the amount of phthalates that come out of these products does not come close to a level of risk."

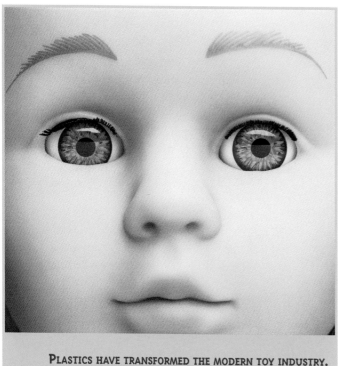

PLASTICS HAVE TRANSFORMED THE MODERN TOY INDUSTRY.

Health questions about Teflon® and the manufacturing process used to make it also continue to raise concerns. While the Environmental Protection Agency (EPA) recognized the potential health dangers of a chemical, perfluorooctanoic acid, known as PFOA or C-8, used to make Teflon®, the safety of the Teflon®-based utensils themselves was not a concern. PFOA is used in manufacturing Teflon® but is not present in the final product. A study by scientists, as reported in *Medical News Today,* demonstrated that "humans are probably exposed to PFOA mainly through drinking water—in miniscule, harmless amounts." Another Teflon® concern has been the fumes given off during cooking. Nonstick cookware such as Teflon® provide a health benefit by requiring the use of either no or a minimum of fat-containing oil. Despite the benefits, there have been reports of small birds dying after ingesting Teflon® cooking fumes. This has been blamed on their small size and delicate breathing systems. Manufacturers also recommend that the cookware never be left unattended. The danger, they say, to humans is negligible, since typical cooking temperatures are usually lower than the 660 degrees Fahrenheit (349 degrees Celsius) at which significant decomposition of Teflon® occurs.

While debate about health and plastics continues, a more visible concern is the effect plastics have had on the environment. Over the decades since the use of plastics became widespread, a major problem has been the disposal of litter and waste. Plastics are durable and degrade slowly. Burning discarded plastic could yield toxic fumes in the air just as the manufacturing of plastics has resulted in the chemical pollution of the air and water.

Pity the whales and other sea animals. As plastics have become a near total presence in our lives, the debris left behind by discarded items—bags, bottles, packaging, fishing nets, and clothing—often ends up in the ocean. This plastic refuse endangers the lives of fish and other sea creatures often causing suffocation, entanglement, or intestinal blockage when discarded plastic is ingested. This has become a worldwide problem. According to the Australian Department of the Environment and Heritage, 6 million tons of debris enters the world's oceans every year, with 18,000 pieces of plastic litter floating on every square mile (2.6 square kilometers) of the world's oceans. Australia's Minister of the Environment and Heritage noted, "Even a fragment of fishing line can cut into the skin of whales, seals or turtles, leading to infection or the slow and painful amputation of flippers, tails or flukes." The department stated that "about one million seabirds and 100,000 marine animals (including 30,000 seals) and turtles are killed by plastic marine litter every year, around the world." After their bodies decay, the cycle continues as the bags or other plastic items they swallowed are released back into the environment ready to be eaten by another animal. While paper towels can take from two to four weeks to break down in the ocean, Styrofoam® cups take fifty years and plastic bottles can take up to 450 years.

In 1991 a zoologist reported to *Nature* magazine that on a visit to a remote and uninhabited Pacific atoll he found large amounts of plastic waste that had washed ashore including crates, bottles, and fishing equipment. "If so much rubbish is washed ashore on small and extremely isolated islands," he concluded, "it makes one wonder just how much more is still floating on the surface of the oceans."

One major solution to the problem of discarded plastics is recycling. The first Earth Day was celebrated in 1970, the same year in which the EPA was established. Both events introduced recycling to consumers who began to realize there was a crisis in solid-waste management. An example was the use of polystyrene (Styrofoam®) cups, dishes, and fast-food containers. These were items that were designed to be used once and then thrown away. Yet, once put in a landfill, they were not biodegradable and were destined to remain intact for decades. One of the largest users of polystyrene packaging was McDonald's. In 1990 the company responded to consumer protests and changed the way it packaged its food products.

Although the concept of recycling is easy to grasp, there are technicalities as far as plastics are concerned. Plastics differ not only in their specific uses but in their ability to be recycled. Containers, for example, can be composed of several different kinds of plastics, and each one needs to be sorted separately before recycling. Plastic waste can be commingled and melted down together, but the resulting dull resin cannot be used freely since the various individual plastic types have differing chemical properties. At the very least they can be turned into plastic lumber or recycling bins but not into more sophisticated products. There are literally thousands of different polymers each with different molecular configurations and properties. Yet only a small number of polymers account for nearly all recycled plastics. Today, recycled plastics are turned into clothing, carpets, playground equipment, and packing materials. You could very well be wearing that soda bottle you recycled months ago. Suppliers to leading clothing manufacturers such as L. L. Bean, Reebok, and Patagonia recycle PET plastic

THE RECYCLING BIN HAS BECOME A FAMILIAR ITEM IN OUR HOMES, SCHOOLS, AND OFFICES.

Resin Identification Codes

1. PETE (or PET): Polyethylene Terephthalate
Soft drink bottles, (PET holds carbonation well), cooking oil bottles, peanut butter jars, medicine bottles, most transparent bottles. Can be recycled into soda bottles, carpets, synthetic textiles, fill for winter coats, and paintbrushes.

2. HDPE: High-density Polyethylene
Detergent bottles, (HDPE can be shaped into bottle handles), milk jugs, sturdy containers. Can be recycled into detergent bottles, irrigation pipes, barrier cones, stadium seats and recycling bins.

3. PVC: Polyvinyl Chloride
Plastic pipes, outdoor furniture, shrink-wrap, salad dressing
liquid detergent containers. Usually not recycled but being used in small amounts to make piping, floor mats, and fencing.

4. LDPE: Low-density Polyethylene
Flexible plastic, dry-cleaning bags, produce bags, trash can liners, food storage, baby bottle liners, bread bags. Not widely recycled but being turned into grocery bags and garbage can liners.

5. PPE: Polypropylene
Pliable plastic, bottle caps, drinking straws, squeeze bottles, yogurt and margarine tubs. Not usually recycled but can be turned into auto parts, ice scrapers, fast food trays, carpets, and textiles.

6. PS: Polystyrene
PS can be formed into either a clear rigid plastic such as salad take-out trays or into a foamed format such as Styrofoam® pellets, cups, plastic tableware, meat trays, take-out food containers. Can be recycled into cafeteria trays, toys, flower pots, trash cans, and DVD cases.

7. OTHER: Other plastics including polycarbonates
Any plastic not numbered 1 through 6, including Tupperware, reusable sports bottles, 5-gallon (18.9-liter) water jugs, and baby bottles. Recyclable, dependent upon the specific plastic.

into polyester making their clothing breathable, wickable, and highly durable. And, when you recycle that clothing, the plastic contents will find yet another use.

By the 1990s, plastic recycling programs had become increasingly common. Both Coca-Cola and Pepsi announced they would begin using plastic bottles containing recycled PET. Thermoplastics could be melted and reused, and thermoset plastics could be ground up and used as filler. Recycling firms have been developing new uses for recycled plastics. In 2000 Conigliaro Industries of Framingham, Massachusetts, started making wall blocks of 50 percent mixed plastics. The blocks are used for retaining walls and to build storage bins and buildings.

The Plastic Bottle Institute devised the now familiar method of marking plastic bottles by type to make them easier to sort for recycling. Of all the many types of plastics in use, only six, according to an article in *E* magazine, account for 97 percent of post-consumer waste. Recyclable plastic containers are often marked on their bottoms with an embossed triangle with three curved arrows containing a number indicating the specific plastic type.

Most plastics today continue to be made from crude oil, petroleum by-products, natural gas, and coal, all nonrenewable natural resources. Concern for the environment, for the growing amount of plastic waste, and about the eventual disappearance of petroleum has led to searches for biodegradable substitutes. Plastics that are biodegradable can be broken down into simpler substances by the activities of living organisms. But the recycling of such plastics cannot take place in traditional landfills but in compost heaps where microbes aided by oxygen and moisture can attack and break them down to their natural states.

Bioplastics are biodegradable, made from renewable raw materials including cellulose, starch—which can be derived from corn, wheat, or potatoes—and soy protein. They are not new. The earliest known plastics were natural resins. John Wesley Hyatt in the 1860s patented a cellulose derivative to make his billiard balls. The use of celluloid led to the development of photographic film and cellophane. In 1941 just

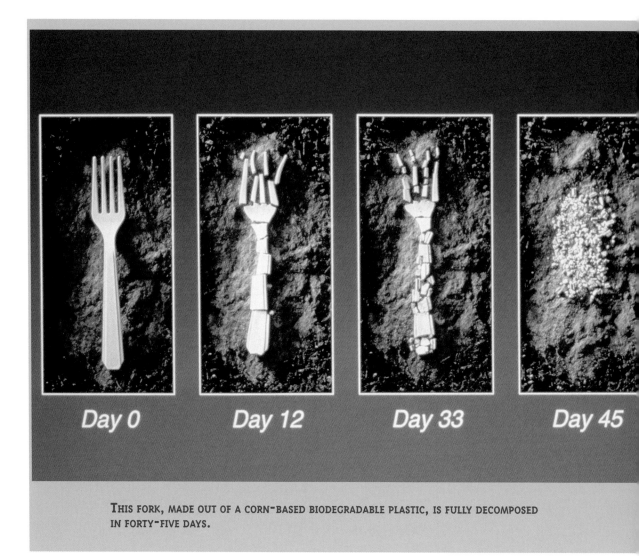

Day 0   Day 12   Day 33   Day 45

THIS FORK, MADE OUT OF A CORN-BASED BIODEGRADABLE PLASTIC, IS FULLY DECOMPOSED IN FORTY-FIVE DAYS.

before the United States entered World War II, Henry Ford developed an experimental plastic automobile body derived from soybeans. The body consisted of fourteen plastic panels fixed to a welded tubular frame and was about two-thirds the weight of a steel model of comparable size.

Biodegradable and compostable plastics are a growing part of the industry, although their costs are still higher than "traditional" plastics. Prices are expected to drop as bioplastics become more popular.

New markets are being constantly opened for this environmentally friendly form. Surgeons can use nontoxic biodegradable polymer sutures, which are initially strong but eventually dissolve and are absorbed by the body. Other uses within the medical world are biodegradable laundry bags, which dissolve in hot wash water and keep contaminated soiled linen away from human contact. There are also agricultural uses in which seeding strips made of degradable plastic and containing regularly spaced seeds and nutrients break down in the soil after the seeds take root.

While we all benefit from modern plastic's variety of uses—from hip replacements and artificial hearts to iPods® and ballpoint pens—we cannot discount the environmental and health concerns. As other forms and uses of plastics emerge and prove to be increasingly indispensable to our way of life, new technologies and new treatments of plastic waste will create the foundation of a bright future for these remarkable and revolutionary materials.

Time Line

1839
Charles Goodyear discovers vulcanization, making rubber tough and springy.

1843
Gutta-percha is introduced to Europe.

1846
Collodion, a sticky mixture of ether alcohol and nitrocellulose, is discovered.

1851
Ebonite, a dark and shiny material formed during vulcanization, is patented. It was the first thermosetting material and was used primarily for jewelry and pens.

1862
Alexander Parkes displays Parkesine, a cellulose nitrate–based product that substituted for ivory or horn. It is highly flammable and brittle.

1868
John Wesley Hyatt produces the first commercial plastic—celluloid.

1869
Hyatt patents the use of collodion for coating billiard balls.

1884 Count Hilaire de Chardonnet spins nitrocellulose into a synthetic silk—a forerunner of rayon, the first synthetic fiber.

1895
Shellac is first used to make phonograph records. It is replaced by PVC in 1948.

1907
Leo Baekeland creates Bakelite, the first synthetic plastic.

1908
Jacques E. Brandenberger invents cellophane.

1912
Thomas Edison invents the Bakelite phonograph record.
Polyvinyl chloride (PVC) is discovered.

1917
Hermann Staudinger discovers that the building blocks of polymers are composed of long chain molecules that repeat themselves.

1927
DuPont begins to market moisture-proof cellophane.

1929
Polystyrene developed in Germany leads to the development of Buna S, a synthetic rubber.

1932
Polyethylene is created accidentally in England.

1935
Nylon is patented by DuPont and Wallace Hume Carothers.

1937
Polyurethane is developed in Germany.

1938
Roy Plunkett of DuPont accidentally discovers PTFE (Teflon®).

1939
The first commercial production of nylon begins in the United States.

1940
"N-Day"—five million pairs of nylon stockings go on sale.

1942
Super Glue is invented and first marketed as a consumer adhesive in 1958.
Polyester fiber production begins.

1943
Silicone is developed, bridging the performance of plastics with rubber.
Silly Putty® is invented by James Wright.

1944
The first polyethylene squeeze bottle is produced.

1948
Velcro® is invented in Switzerland by George de Mestral.

1949
The first plastic Lego® blocks appear.

1950
Acrylic fiber is produced commercially for the first time.

1951
Tupperware is introduced as a full product line.

1952
"Wash and wear" clothes go on sale.

1953
Polyester fiber is commercially produced in the United States for the first time.

1953
The Chevrolet Corvette is the first production automobile with an all-fiberglass body.

1957
The first plastic sandwich bags are made.
The Monsanto House of the Future opens at Disneyland.

1958
The hula hoop is introduced.

1959
The first Barbie® doll appears.
Lycra is invented.

1965
Kevlar® is invented by Stephanie Kwolek.

1966
The first plastic produce bags, contained on a roll, are introduced in grocery stores.

1969
Neil Armstrong plants a nylon American flag on the moon.

1977
The first plastic grocery bags are introduced to supermarkets.

1982
The first artificial heart is implanted.

1996
The U.S. Food and Drug Administration approves polymer wafer implants for treating brain cancer.

Bakelite—A thermoset plastic made of phenol and formaldehyde with a wood flour filler that is molded under heat and pressure. It was the first synthetic plastic.

Bakelizer—The steam pressure vessel used by Leo Baekeland to create Bakelite, the first synthetic plastic. The original is now at the National Museum of American History in Washington, D.C.

bioplastics—A new generation of biodegradable plastics made from renewable raw materials such as starch and cellulose.

blow molding—A process used to create hollow plastic shapes.

Buna S—An early synthetic rubber developed in Germany.

casein—A milk by-product used to manufacture plastic items such as knife handles, buttons, and beads.

Catalin™—A trademarked plastic which, like Bakelite, is made of phenolics. Its bright colors made it popular as radio cabinets.

cellophane—A thin transparent sheet made of cellulose. The clear film is used in packaging and with applied adhesive as a tape.

celluloid—The first thermoplastic, made of nitrocellulose and camphor. It is easily moldable but highly flammable.

collodion—A product created by dissolving cellulose nitrate in ether and alcohol. It was first used as a protective covering for wounds.

cracking—A process in the refining of petroleum in which hydrocarbon molecules are broken up into lighter molecules suitable for creating raw materials which are, in turn, used to create plastic feedstocks.

DEHA—Commonly used as a plasticizer to create plastic food wrap; the acronym stands for diethylhydroxylamine.

extrusion—A process in which a variety of molded parts are created by melting, heating, and pumping plastics resins by the use of one or more screws.

feedstock—Raw materials, chemical or petroleum based, used to make plastics.

gutta-percha—A natural gum from trees grown in Malaysia, Borneo, and Sumatra. It is a natural plastic widely used in the nineteenth century as a waterproof nonbrittle insulation of marine cables.

HDPE—High-density polyethylene, a plastic used to make bottles, milk jugs, and margarine and garbage containers.

injection molding—A process in which melted plastic resin is injected into a mold to create a finished product.

LDPE—Low-density polyethylene, a tough and flexible plastic used in the making of grocery bags, dry-cleaner bags, lids, and bottles.

monomer—A single molecule that can combine with molecules to form a polymer.

nylon—The first synthetic fiber made entirely of coal, water, and air. Originally used as a replacement for silk.

Parkesine™—A trademarked product and the first synthetic plastic (pyroxlin) made from cellulose, nitric acid, and a solvent.

PFOA— Perfluorooctanoic acid, a synthetic chemical essential to make the fluoropolymers used to make Teflon®-coated nonstick cookware.

phthalates—Chemical compounds used as plasticizers and which increase the flexibility of plastics.

plastic—Any high-polymeric substance, including natural and synthetic products, capable of flowing under heat and pressure to create a final shape.

plasticizers—Substances added to plastics to increase their flexibility.

polyurethane—Used in flexible and rigid foams and to make seals, gaskets, and hard plastic parts. It can be made in a wide range of hardnesses and have high-impact resistance.

polymer—A molecule composed of repeated smaller molecules of the same substance. Plastics are polymers.

PET— Polyethylene terephtalate, a thermoplastic polymer resin used to create synthetic fibers. It is the basis for such fibers as polyester and dacron. Can be semirigid to rigid depending on thickness. Used for beverage, food, and liquid containers.

PP—Polypropylene, a versatile thermoplastic resin with a high melting point. It is strong and chemically resistant and can be molded into a variety of shapes.

PS—Polystyrene, a strong plastic with a low melting point, it can be injected, extruded, or blow-molded to make containers, cups, bottles, now in DVD cases, and plastic cutlery.

Plexiglas®—A lightweight, transparent, weather-resistant thermoplastic that can be molded and used in windows as a substitute for glass.

PVC—Polyvinyl chloride, a familiar plastic as vinyl siding, credit cards, and pipelines. When plasticizers are added to make it softer and flexible, it can be used in clothing and upholstery.

rayon—Not a true synthetic since it is made from cellulose. Originally, it was a substitute for silk.

resin—A clear or translucent substance used in producing plastics. It is the "raw" form of plastic.

rotational molding—A process of turning plastic powder into useful hollow products.

Saran®—Also known as polyvinylidene chloride, a plastic film, primarily used to protect food and provide a barrier to oxygen, moisture, and heat. Saran Wrap is a trademark of the Dow Chemical Company.

shellac—A secretion of the lac beetle used to make a protective coating for wood. It was able to be molded and was used to manufacture early phonograph records.

spinneret—A multiholed device through which plastic polymer melt is extruded to form fibers. Streams of syrupy polymer exit metal nozzles and solidify in the cold air to form synthetic fiber.

silicone rubber—A flexible plastic that can be easily shaped and molded. It can repel water but has strong bonding capabilities and slipperiness.

Styrofoam®—The trademarked name for a form of insulation foam made by the Dow Chemical Company. Popularly used as cups, food containers, and packaging material.

Teflon®—A trademark of the DuPont Company for fluorocarbon resins used for nonstick cookware.

thermoplastics—Plastics that can be repeatedly softened and heated to created new products.

thermosets—Plastics that cannot be re-formed through heating and cooling. Bakelite is an example.

viscose—A synthetic fiber composed of cellulose fibers from wood, cotton, or hemp dissolved in alkali.

Velcro®—A trademark for a brand of hook-and-loop fasteners.

vulcanization—A linking together, under heat and pressure with sulfur, of rubber compound polymers which alter the chemical structure of rubber into a substance that is elastic and bouncy. The process made automobile tires possible.

Web Sites

http://www.americanplasticscouncil.org
For general information about plastics.

http://www.teachingplastics.org
Educational information for students and teachers.

http://www.plasticsinfo.org
A focus on plastics and health.

http://www.plasticsresource.com
A focus on plastics and the environment.

http://www.nationalgeographic.com/education/plastics
A useful site for students.

Bibliography

Books

Clarke, Alison J. *Tupperware: The Promise of Plastic in 1950s America.* Washington, DC: Smithsonian Institution Press, 1999.

Fenichell, Stephen. *Plastic: The Making of a Synthetic Century.* New York: HarperBusiness, 1996.

Meikle, Jeffrey L. *American Plastic: A Cultural History.* New Brunswick, NJ: Rutgers University Press, 1995.

Roberts, Royston M. *Serendipity: Accidental Discoveries in Science.* New York: Wiley, 1989.

Sparke, Penny. *The Plastic Age.* Woodstock, NY: Overlook Press, 1992.

Places to Visit

Hagley Museum and Library
PO Box 3630
Wilmington, DE 19807

National Plastics Center and Museum
210 Lancaster Street
Leominster, MA 01453
http://www.plasticsmuseum.org

Index

Page numbers for illustrations are in **boldface**.

Acknowledgments

I wish to thank the following for cheerfully sharing their knowledge and information, which have enriched this book:

Barbara D. Hall and Jon Williams at the Hagley Museum and Library, Wilmington, Delaware, for the invaluable resources of the DuPont archives; Keith Lauer at the National Plastics Center and Museum, Leominster, Massachusetts, for his deep insight into the history of early plastics; Abraham Lastnik, formerly of the U.S. Army Natick Research, Development, and Engineering Center, Natick, Massachusetts, for providing technical insight; Alan Vivat, Boston, Massachusetts, for his first-hand accounts of early plastics consumerism; Al Cooper, NYPRO Plastics, Clinton, Massachusetts, for his expert tour of a modern plastics-manufacturing plant; Debbie Levey, Massachusetts Institute of Technology, for information about the Monsanto House of the Future.

I am also indebted to the following for providing answers to research questions: Tupperware, DuPont, GE Plastics, Bayer, Wham-O, Lego Systems, U.S. Environmental Protection Agency, U.S. Food and Drug Administration, and the Library of Congress. I am especially grateful to the American Plastics Council for information that enhances this book.

And for the use of copyrighted material: "You're the Top"
Music and lyrics by Cole Porter ©1934 Warner Bros. Inc. (Renewed) All Rights Reserved. Lyrics reprinted with the permission of Warner Bros. Publications, Miami, FL 33014

I am especially indebted to my wife, Rosalind, for her patience and editorial insight.

About the Author

Norman H. Finkelstein is a retired school librarian and teacher. He is the author of fourteen nonfiction books for young readers and is the recipient of two National Jewish Book Awards and the Golden Kite Honor Award for Nonfiction. He is a member of the Authors Guild and the Society of Children's Book Writers and Illustrators. For further information, visit his Web site: http://www.normfinkelstein.com